MATHEMATICS

for

Plumbers

and

Pipefitters

MATHEMATICS

for

Plumbers

and

Pipefitters

DELMAR PUBLISHERS
COPYRIGHT © 1973
BY LITTON EDUCATIONAL PUBLISHING, INC.

LIBRARY OF CONGRESS CATALOG CARD NUMBER: 73-2166

PRINTED IN THE UNITED STATES OF AMERICA

Bartholomew D'Arcangelo
Benedict D'Arcangelo
J. Russell Guest

DELMAR PUBLISHERS • ALBANY, NEW YORK 12205

A DIVISION OF LITTON EDUCATIONAL PUBLISHING, INC.

Preface

Mathematics for Plumbers and Pipefitters was developed to fill a need for a specialized course to meet the particular requirements of those in the plumbing and pipefitting trades. The emphasis, therefore, has been placed upon the development of usable skills in the layout, measurement, and computation of pipe lengths. The current revision extends coverage to meet recent innovations in the field.

The modern plumber must be able to plan his work rather than use a cut-and-fit method of pipe fitting. He must be able to take measurements for several pipes and cut them either on the job or in the shop. Some plumbing firms cut all the pipe in the shop from pipe diagrams and measurements made on the job by the plumber. All the possibilities need to be at the plumber's command so that he may use the adaptability of various degree fittings to best avoid obstacles. He must be aware of and able to adapt new materials and techniques.

The authors who developed this instructional material have a wide background of experience in plumbing instruction in both day trade and apprentice programs in Buffalo, New York.

• Bartholomew D'Arcangelo, former Instructor, Plumbing Trades, is a member and former officer of Plumbers Local #36, Buffalo N.Y., The United Association of Journeymen and Apprentices of the Plumbing and Pipefitting Industry of the United States and Canada.

• Benedict D'Arcangelo, Instructor, Plumbing Trades, member and also officer of the above union, Plumbers Local #36, has had wide experience as Estimator and Supervisor of Plumbing in the Buffalo area.

• J. Russell Guest, Instructor, Related Subjects, is a qualified mechanical engineer who has served as a Curriculum Specialist with the New York State Education Department on a number of curriculum projects developed in cooperation with the Buffalo Board of Education.

The author and editorial staff at Delmar Publishers are interested in continually improving the quality of this instructional material. The reader is invited to submit constructive criticism and questions. Responses will be reviewed jointly by the author and source editor.

Editor-in-Chief
Delmar Publishers
50 Wolf Road
Albany, New York 12205

Contents

SECTION IV   VOLUMES, PRESSURE, CAPACITIES

SECTION V   HEATING

SECTION VI   THE BUILDER'S LEVEL

APPENDIX

Unit 1   RULES FOR MATHEMATICAL SHORTHAND

RELATED INFORMATION

Before proceeding to the trade applications which comprise the bulk of this book, it is well to review those fundamentals which must be mastered in order to solve mathematical problems in the pipe trades. This is the first of six units which summarize these basic principles and serve as a refresher before applications to the trade are made.

Mathematics has its own system of shorthand which must be thoroughly understood in order to solve problems. This shorthand consists of signs and symbols which have definite and unchanging meanings. The following are the most important of these signs and symbols for the plumber or pipefitter to master:

Mathematical Shorthand	Arithmetic Form	Formula Form
ADD: Use plus sign as 8 + 5, or B + b	7 + 6, or 7 + 6	a + b, 7 + c
SUBTRACT: Use dash as 8 - 5, or k - m	8 - 5, or 8 - 5	a - b, 7 - c, d - 3
MULTIPLY: Use cross with numbers as 8 × 5. Use no sign with letters as ab, which reads 'a times b'	8 × 5, or 8 × 5	ab, 7c
DIVIDE: Use division sign, division bracket, or fraction bar.	8 ÷ 5 5) 8 $\frac{8}{5}$	$\frac{a}{b}$, $\frac{c}{3}$, $\frac{4}{d}$
SQUARE: Use exponent two.	$8^2 = 8 \times 8$	$a^2 = a \times a = aa$
CUBE: Use exponent three.	$8^3 = 8 \times 8 \times 8$	$a^3 = a \times a \times a = aaa$
SQUARE ROOT: Use radical sign	$\sqrt{25}$	$\sqrt{a}$, $\sqrt{a^2 + b^2}$

GROUPING NUMBERS

1. Parentheses ( ), or brackets [ ], mean that two or more numbers are to be treated as one. For practical purposes, it indicates to do the work in parentheses first. 2 (a + b) reads two times the sum of a plus b. 2 a + b reads two times a plus b. If a = 5 and b = 6, 2 (a + b) = 2 (5 + 6) = 22. 2 a + b = 10 + 6 = 16.

2. A long division bar groups numbers.

$$\frac{a + b}{5}$$ means that both a and b are divided by 5

However, $\frac{a}{5}$ + b means that only 'a' is divided by 5

Again, if a = 5, b = 6, $\frac{a + b}{5} = \frac{5 + 6}{5} = \frac{11}{5} = 2\frac{1}{5}$

But, $\frac{5}{5}$ + 6 = 1 + 6 = 7

3. A long radical bar as $\sqrt{a^2 + b^2}$ requires the square root of the <u>sum</u> <u>of</u> the two squares.

SAMPLE PROBLEMS

In each equation, a = 4, b = 5, c = 6. Solve each for a number answer.

1. a + b - c = x

    4 + 5 - 6 = x

    3 = x   <u>Ans.</u>

2. $\frac{ab}{c}$ = y

    $\frac{4 \times 5}{6}$ = y $6\overline{)20}^{\,3\ 1/3}$

    3 1/3 = y   <u>Ans.</u>

3. 2 (a + b) = m

    2 (4 + 5) = m

    2 × 9 = m

    18 = m   <u>Ans.</u>

4. 2 a + b = n

    2 × 4 + b = n

    8 + 5 = n

    13 = n   <u>Ans.</u>

5. $\frac{7 + a}{2}$ = p

    $\frac{7 + 4}{2}$ = p

    $\frac{11}{2}$ = p

    5 1/2 = p   <u>Ans.</u>

6. $\frac{7}{2}$ + a = q

    $\frac{7}{2}$ + 4 = q

    3.5 + 4 = q

    7.5 = q   <u>Ans.</u>

2

ASSIGNMENT

Solve each of the following, using f = 8, g = 9, and h = 10.

1. h + f = a   _____

2. h - g = b   _____

3. hfg = c   _____

4. $\dfrac{gf}{h}$ = d   _____

5. 2f + 3g + 4h = x   _____

6. f^2 + 3g = y   _____

7. $\sqrt{g}$ + $\dfrac{h}{3}$ = m   _____

8. $\dfrac{(f + h)}{2}$ g = A   _____

9. 3 (h - f) = n   _____

10. $\dfrac{(fg)^2}{h}$ = p   _____

Unit 2 FORMULAS

RELATED INFORMATION

Problem-solving in the pipe trades requires a sound knowledge of length, area and volume formulas and how they are applied. A formula is simply a rule expressed with symbols instead of words. For example, the rule for finding the area of a rectangle is to multiply the length by the width. In a formula, we express length as L, width as W, and area as A. (Any other letters would do just as well so long as the letter and what it refers to are clearly identified). Stating the rule in formula form, then, A = LW.

Many of the following formulas are familiar to you. They are presented here as a refresher and later in the course each will be applied to specific problems of the pipe trades.

Length Formula	Geometric Shape	Area Formula
P = perimeter S = side P = 4S	SQUARE	A = area A = S^2
L = length W = width P = 2L + 2W or P = 2 (L + W)	RECTANGLE	A = LW
C = circumference π = 3.14* d = diameter r = radius C = πd	CIRCLE	A = πr^2 or A = .7854 d^2

* π = 3.1416, but for practical purposes, the plumber
should use the abbreviated form shown.

Length Formula	Geometric Shape	Area Formula

$$c = \sqrt{a^2 + b^2}$$

$$P = a + b + c$$

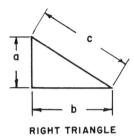

RIGHT TRIANGLE

$$A = \frac{ab}{2}$$

$$P = a + b + c$$

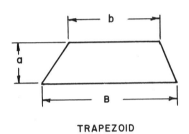

ANY TRIANGLE

$$A = \frac{ab}{2}$$

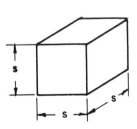

TRAPEZOID

$$A = \frac{(B + b)\,a}{2}$$

Volume Formula

CUBE

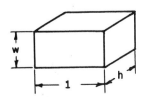

$$V = S^3$$

RECTANGULAR PRISM

$$V = lwh$$

TRIANGULAR PRISM 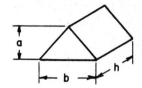 $$V = \frac{a\,b\,h}{2}$$

TRAPEZOIDAL PRISM 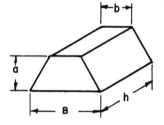 $$V = \frac{(B + b)}{2}\,a\,h$$

CYLINDER 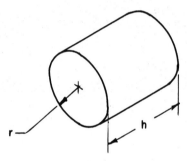 $$V = \pi r^2 h$$

SAMPLE PROBLEMS

1. Compute the circumference of a round pipe with a diameter of 6 1/2 inches.

   6 1/2 inches

   $C = \pi d$

   $C = 3.14 \times 6.5$

   $C = 20.41$ inches   Ans.

2. Compute the area of shape in sketch.

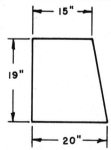

$$A = \frac{(B + b)\,a}{2}$$

$$A = \frac{(20 + 15)}{2} \times 19$$

$$A = \frac{35}{2} \times 19$$

$$A = 332.5 \text{ square inches} \quad \text{Ans.}$$

3. Compute the volume of a cylinder 14″ in diameter and 20″ long.

$$V = \pi r^2 h$$

$$V = 3.14 \times 7 \times 7 \times 20$$

$$V = 3077.20 \text{ cubic inches} \quad \underline{\text{Ans.}}$$

ASSIGNMENT

A. Solve for each length.

1. Perimeter of a room 12′-6″ × 12′-6″.   _____

2. Perimeter of a room 18′-9″ × 15′-0″.   _____

3. Circumference of a pipe 12 3/4″ diameter.   _____

B. Solve for each area.

1. The square inches of copper in a sheet 14 1/2″ × 14 1/2″.   _____

2. The square feet of lead in a sheet 3′-6″ × 4′-6″.   _____

3. The square feet in a house gable 26′-0″ × 9′-0″.   _____

4. The square inches of opening in a trapezoid-shaped hole with parallel lines 14″ and 22″ that are 12″ apart.   _____

5. Area of a circle 18″ in diameter.   _____

C. Solve for each volume.

1. The cubic inches in a cube 12″ on a side.   _____

2. The cubic yards for a cellar hole 30′-0″ × 36′-0″ × 4′-6″ deep.   _____

3. The cubic feet of an attic 8′-0″ high for a 24′-0″ × 34′-0″ house.   _____

4. The cubic inches for a cylindrical pail 9″ in diameter and 11″ high.   _____

Unit 3 TRANSPOSITION

RELATED INFORMATION

Transposition means, literally, "cross-position". It is a process for re-arranging a formula in the manner best suited for a specific problem. For instance, we know that the perimeter of a square equals four times the length of one side or P = 4S. If one side is 10″, P = 40″. Suppose we know that P = 36″ and wish to find S. By transposing the formula P = 4S into S = P ÷ 4, we find S equals 9″.

Briefly, the rule for transposition is that a number moved across the equal sign takes the opposite arithmetic; that is, add (+) becomes subtract (-), multiply (×) becomes divide (÷), and vice versa.

SAMPLE PROBLEMS

1. D - 7 = 10.   Find D.

    Transpose (-7).   D = 10 + 7 = 17.

2. D + 7 = 10.   Find D.

    Transpose (+7).   D = 10 - 7 = 3.

3. $\frac{D}{7}$ = 15.   Find D.

    Transpose (divided by 7).   D = 15 × 7 = 105.

4. 8D = 72

    Transpose (8×).   D = 72 ÷ 8 = 9.

Squares and radicals also take opposite arithmetic when moved across the equal sign. The numbers, however, are not moved. When transposed, $\sqrt{\ }$ becomes $(\ )^2$ and $(\ )^2$ becomes $\sqrt{\ }$.

5. $\sqrt{m}$ = 5.   Find m.   Square both sides.

$$\sqrt{m}^2 = 5^2$$
$$m = 5^2$$
$$m = 25$$

6. d^2 = 100.   Find d.   Take square root of both sides.

$$\sqrt{d^2} = \sqrt{100}$$
$$d = \sqrt{100}$$
$$d = 10$$

8

ASSIGNMENT

Solve each of the following problems, using transposition.

1. A square room has an area of 225 square feet. How long
    is one side?   _____

2. A square plot has a perimeter of 66 feet. How long is one
    side?   _____

3. A circle has a circumference of 22 inches. Compute the
    diameter.   _____

4. How wide is a piece of sheet lead 30 inches long if the area
    is 144 square inches?   _____

5. A circle has an area of 50.24 square inches. How long is
    the radius and how long is the diameter?   _____

                                                              _____

Unit 4   SQUARE ROOT

RELATED INFORMATION

"Taking the square root" of a number means determining what number multiplied by itself will give the original number. What number multiplied by itself will give 4? Obviously, 2×2. So, 2 is the square root of 4.

Square root is often used in solving for the "hypotenuse" of a right triangle. The hypotenuse is the side opposite the right angle. Diagonals in pipe assemblies represent this hypotenuse.

SAMPLE PROBLEM

Solve for the length of the hypotenuse "c".

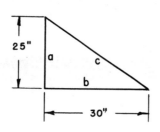

$$c = \sqrt{a^2 + b^2}$$

$$c = \sqrt{625 + 900}$$

$$c = \sqrt{1525}$$

$$c = 39.05''$$

$$c = 39\ 1/16''\quad \underline{\text{Ans.}}$$

SQUARE ROOT SOLUTION

1. Locate the decimal point.

$$\sqrt{1525.}$$

2. Pair off both ways from the decimal point.

$$\sqrt{15\ 25.00\ 00}$$

3. Examine the first pair under the radical sign (15) and determine the approximate square root. In this case, the square root is more than 3 but less than 4 because $3 \times 3 = 9$ and $4 \times 4 = 16$.

$$\sqrt{15}$$

4. Place the 3 outside the radical sign above the 15. Multiply the 3 by itself and place the product (9) under the 15.

$$\overset{3}{\sqrt{15}}$$
$$\underline{9}$$

10

5. Subtract as in a division problem to get the remainder.

6. Carry down the next pair of numbers (25) and add to the remainder.

7. Double the answer number, 3, to use as a trial divisor and write the 6 outside the division frame in the tens column.

8. Determine how many times the "sixty-something" may be divided into 625. The number in the unit column must be the same as that used as a multiplier. In this case, try 9. Place it in the answer and after the 6 in the divisor. 69×9 is 621. Place this under the 625.

9. Subtract and bring down the next pair of numbers (00).

10. Again, double the present answer (39) as a trial divisor for 400. Place the result (78) in the hundreds and tens columns.

11. How many times will "seven hundred eighty-something" go into 400? Obviously, none, as it is already larger. So, place a zero in your answer above the two zeros after the decimal point. Place a zero after the 78 in the trial divisor to become 780 and bring down the next pair of numbers (00).

12. Now, as in Step 8, what number can be added to the 780 and be used as a multiplier to get 40000? $\underline{5} \times 780\underline{5} = 39025$.

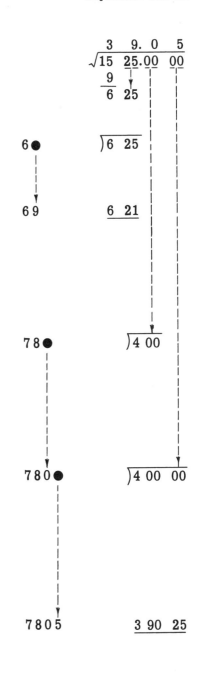

The $\sqrt{1525} = 39.05$ correct to two decimal places.

NOTE: Steps 1, 2, 3, and 4 are used once in each problem.

   Steps 5, 6, 7, and 8 show how each number in the answer is obtained after the first one.

   Step 11 shows the use of zero in the answer.

FACTORING METHOD

The preceding step-by-step procedure for extracting the square root of a number can sometimes be simplified or bypassed. Such a shortcut is possible if the number under the radical sign can be broken down into numbers whose square root is already known or can be found more easily. This method is called factoring.

Example: Find $\sqrt{400}$

1. Break the number into numbers whose square roots are known. $\sqrt{4} \times \sqrt{100}$

2. Extract the square root of each factor. 2×10

3. Multiply the factors. 20

This same method could be employed with 1525.

$$1525 = \sqrt{15.25} \times \sqrt{100} \qquad \text{Thus, } 10 \times \sqrt{15.25}$$

In this case we must still find the square root of 15.25 and multiply the answer by 10.

USE OF SQUARE ROOT TABLES

Square Root Tables for numbers 1.000 to 99.90 are included in the Appendix.

Excerpt of Table C Appendix

	0	1	2	3
14.	3.742	3.755	3.768	3.782
15.	3.873	3.886	3.899	3.912
16.	4.000	4.012	4.025	4.037
17.	4.123	4.135	4.147	4.159
18.	4.243	4.254	4.266	4.278

1. Read 15.2 and 15.3 on Table C which covers numbers 10 through 54.9.

2. The square root of 15.25 may be estimated as the average of the two answers:

$$\sqrt{15.2} = 3.899$$
$$\sqrt{15.3} = \underline{3.912}$$
$$7.811 \div 2 = 3.905$$

3. $\sqrt{1525} = \sqrt{100 \times 15.25} = 10 \times 3.905 = 39.05$

ASSIGNMENT

A. Solve for the hypotenuse (c) in each of the right triangles.

	a	b	c
1.	6″	8″	
2.	8″	15″	
3.	20″	25″	
4.	27″	32″	
5.	44″	19″	
6.	12″	12″	
7.	1″	1″	
8.	10″	11 1/4″	
9.	9 1/2″	16″	
10.	17 1/2″	23 1/4″	

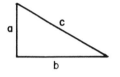

B. Solve for the altitude (a) in each of the right triangles.

NOTE: Transpose the formula $c^2 = a^2 + b^2$

	a	b	c
1.		12″	15″
2.		2″	3″
3.		13″	18″
4.		24″	25″
5.		6″	40″

Unit 5 REVIEW OF ANGLE MEASURE

RELATED INFORMATION

Ancient Egyptian astronomers devised angle measure. They thought themselves at the center of a circle with the sun rising and setting on different points of the circumference. The vertex of an angle is the center of a circle and the angle is formed by radius lines.

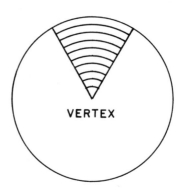

VERTEX

THE DEGREES OF A CIRCLE

The Egyptians set the number of degrees for a circle at 360 as their year had 360 work days and five feast days. The 360° circle angle has continued in use. A degree is 1/360 of a full circle angle.

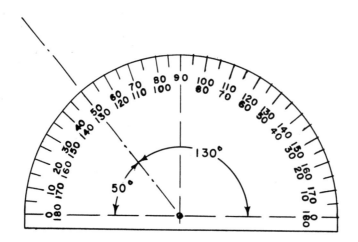

THE PROTRACTOR

The protractor is used to measure or construct angles. The center point of the protractor must be at the vertex of the angle. One of the radius lines is located along the base line of the protractor. The second radius line is located at a number of degrees from the first. The protractor has two rows of numbers so that angles can be measured clockwise (outer numbers) or counter clockwise (inner numbers). The length of the radius lines do not affect the angle measure between them.

THE STRAIGHT ANGLE

Two lines that meet to form a straight line are at an angle of 180°, or half a circle angle.

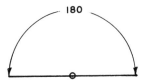

THE RIGHT ANGLE

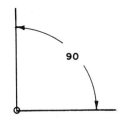

The right angle (or correct angle) is formed in building construction by a vertical line meeting a horizontal line. A right angle is 90° which is one-fourth of a circle angle.

THE SUM OF ANGLES IN A TRIANGLE

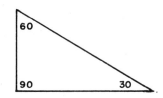
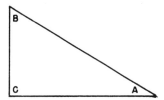

The three angles in any triangle add to 180°. Angle A plus angle B plus angle C equals 180°.

OPPOSITE ANGLES

When two lines cross the opposite angles are equal.

Angle A = Angle B

Angle C = Angle D

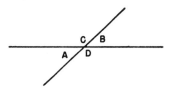

ALTERNATE ANGLES

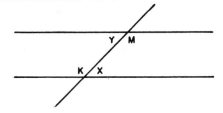

When parallel lines are crossed by a third line, the alternate interior angles are equal.

Angle X = Angle Y

Angle K = Angle M

SAMPLE PROBLEM

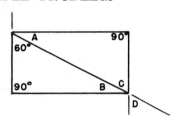

Solve for the degrees for each lettered angle. State the basis for your method.

1. Angle C = 60°   Alternate angles are equal.

2. Angle A = 30°   180° - (60 + 90) = 30°
                                    Sum of 3 angles = 180°

3. Angle B = Angle A = 30°   Alternate angles are equal.

4. Angle D = Angle C = 60°   Opposite angles are equal.

ASSIGNMENT

1. a. Use a protractor to make a figure similar to the sample problem, using a 48° angle in place of the 60° angle.

    b. Measure each angle with a protractor and write down your readings.

    _____

    _____

    c. Solve for each angle and compare with angle measurements.

    _____

    _____

    _____

    _____

2. Read the values of the angles indicated by each letter:

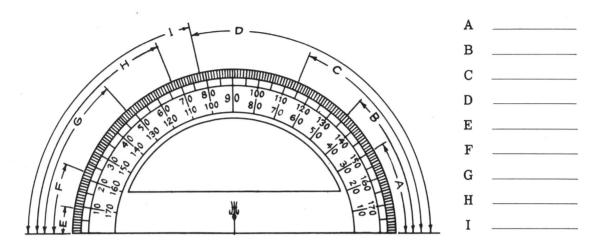

A _____

B _____

C _____

D _____

E _____

F _____

G _____

H _____

I _____

3. Measure the angles below with a protractor:

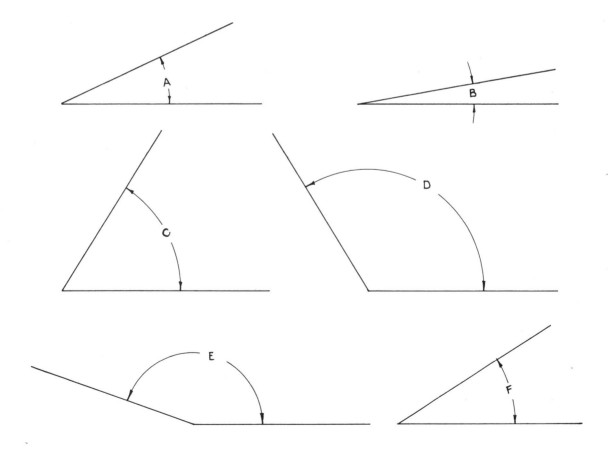

Unit 6   CONVERSION OF LENGTH MEASURES

RELATED INFORMATION

Dimensions are better tools when they are in the form which best suits the particular problem. In some cases, dimensions in feet and inches may be easiest to work with; in others, inches alone may be best. Calculations are often best figured in decimals, but need to be converted to feet and inches for measuring purposes. The recommended dimension form for various problems is used in each unit of this book. This unit covers methods of converting from one form to another.

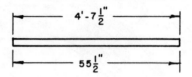

There are four standard methods of graduating measuring tools: (1) inches and fractional parts of an inch; (2) inches and decimal parts of an inch; (3) feet, inches and fractions; (4) feet and decimal parts of a foot.

The plumber's rule reads in inches and sixteenth-inches. The steel tape reads in inches and eighth-inches. Rules are made in inches and decimal parts, although decimal inches are generally confined to calculations in plumbing. Surveyors and architects often use feet and decimal parts of a foot for land measure.

SAMPLE PROBLEMS

1. Fractional inches to decimal inches.

   Change $\frac{11''}{16}$ to decimal inches. $\frac{11}{16}$ is 11 divided by 16

   $\frac{11''}{16}$ = .6875"   <u>Ans.</u>

2. Decimal inches to nearest sixteenth inch.

   Change .725" to nearest 16th inch.

   $.725'' \times \frac{16}{16} = \frac{11.6}{16} = \frac{12}{16} = \frac{3''}{4}$ <u>Ans.</u>

3. Feet to inches.

   Change 8'-5" to inches.   8' = 96" + 5" = 101"   <u>Ans.</u>

4. Feet to inches.

   Change .69' to inches.   .69 feet × 12 = 8.28 inches   <u>Ans.</u>

5. Inches to feet and inches.

Change 110″ to feet and inches.   110″ ÷ 12 = 9′-2″   **Ans.**

6. Inches to decimal foot.

Change 11 1/2″ to feet.   11 1/2″ = 11.5 ÷ 12 = .958′   **Ans.**

7. Feet to inches and nearest sixteenth inch.

Change 1.78 feet so it can be measured on rule.

$$1.78' \times 12'' = 21.36'' \qquad .36'' \times \frac{16}{16} = \frac{3''}{8}$$

$$1.78' = 21 \, 3/8'' \quad \textbf{Ans.}$$

ASSIGNMENT

Compute each length into the form indicated by the column heading.

	Inches and Fractional Parts of Inch	Inches and Decimal Parts of Inch	Feet, Inches, and Fractional Parts of Inch	Feet and Decimal Parts of Foot
1.	$19 \frac{11''}{16}$			
2.		26.35″		
3.			$8'-4\frac{1''}{2}$	
4.				5.57′
5.		103.72″		

Section II PIPE LENGTH CALCULATIONS

Unit 7 STANDARD WEIGHT PIPE

RELATED INFORMATION

Pipe is made in three weights: standard, extra heavy and double extra heavy.

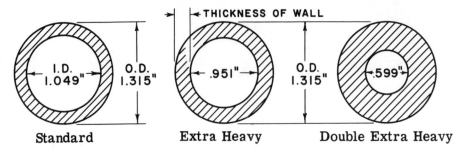

Standard   Extra Heavy   Double Extra Heavy

The cross sections show the inside and outside diameters for the three weights in 1" nominal size pipe. The outside diameters are alike so that the same threading dies will fit all three weights of pipe. The water pressure determines the weight of pipe needed. Most plumbing is done with standard weight pipe.

NOMINAL SIZE

Nominal or name size of pipe is based on the inside diameter. Manufacturing changes over the years have enlarged the inside diameter of small sizes so that the I.D. of 1/8" pipe is more than 1/4". (See Data #1, Appendix)

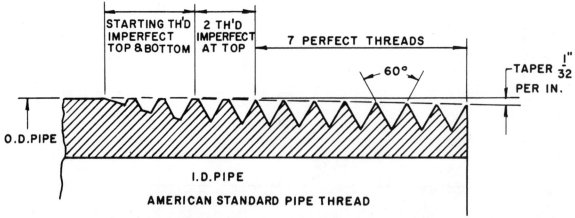

AMERICAN STANDARD PIPE THREAD

The American National Pipe thread has a slight taper so that tightening the pipe into a fitting has a wedging action. All the threads cut on the pipe cannot be used as the starting threads are not full or perfect threads. Some dies have an adjustment for thread depth. A properly threaded pipe will turn by hand 3 to 4 threads into a fitting.

20

SAMPLE PROBLEM

Compute the maximum clearance between a 1/2" pipe and the wood auger hole as shown in Data #1, Appendix.

SOLUTION

Step 1: Determine diameter of wood auger hole
        required for 1/2" pipe (Data #1)   =   15/16"

Step 2: Determine O.D. of 1/2" pipe (Data #1)   =   .840

Step 3: Convert decimal to fraction (16ths)
                    .840 × 16   =   13.44 or 13/16"

Step 4: Subtract O.D. of 1/2" pipe from diameter
        of auger hole.   15/16" - 13/16"   =   1/8" clearance
                                                           Ans.

ASSIGNMENT

Answer the following questions based on Data #1, Appendix.

1. Compute the maximum clearance between a 3/4" pipe and the
    wood auger hole.   _____

2. Compute the same for 1", 2 1/2", and 6" pipe.   _____

                                                               _____

                                                               _____

3. What is a tap drill? _____
    Why is it smaller than the O.D. of the pipe?_____

    _____

    _____

4. How far will a 2 1/2" pipe advance into a fitting with one full turn?   _____

5. How far will a 1" pipe advance into a fitting with one full turn?   _____

Unit 8   ALLOWANCE FOR FITTINGS

RELATED INFORMATION

Pipe length is measured along the center lines. When two center lines cross there is a center point. These center points are located in a fitting. Center-to-center and end-to-center measurements are often made on the job. The pipe is cut to an end-to-end length. The end-to-end is always shorter than the center-to-center because the pipe does not thread into a fitting as far as the center point. The illustration shows various ways of measuring pipe.

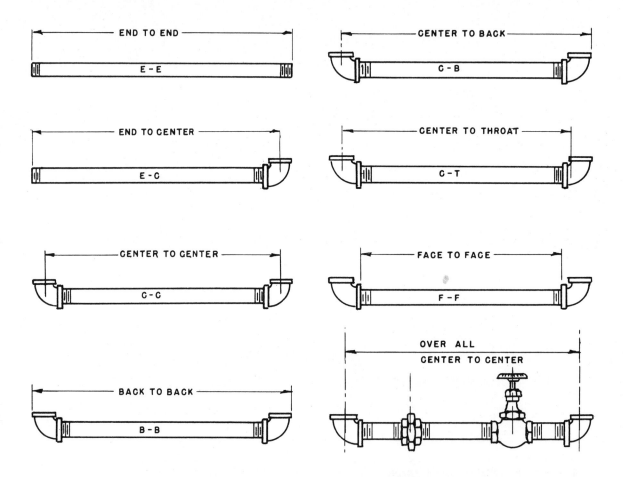

The length to cut threaded pipe cannot be measured directly. It is necessary to make an allowance for fittings. This allowance provides space for the fitting and for the pipe to thread into the fitting to make the connection.

Threaded fittings are not standardized except in thread dimensions.   The center-to-face measurement varies with manufacturers. Also, there are long and short patterns of fittings. On the job, measure the fitting.

Data Sheets #2, 3, 4, and 5, Appendix, show center-to-face (C-F) measurements for use with the problems of this book.   These tables were made by measuring fittings in the shop.

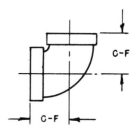

SAMPLE PROBLEM

Solve for e-e length.

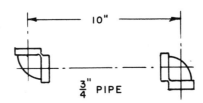

Step 1:   Center-to-face measurement for 3/4″
90° ell, using Data #2, Appendix   =   1 3/8″
Two ells   =   2 3/4″ (To subtract from
c-c)

Step 2:   Thread-in for 3/4″ 90° ell, using Data
#2, Appendix   =   1/2″
Two thread-ins   =   1″ (To add to e-e length)

Step 3:   2 3/4″ - 1″ = 1 3/4″ to be subtracted from c-c length.

Step 4:   10″ - 1 3/4″ = 8 1/4″ e-e   **Ans.**

ASSIGNMENT

Solve Problems 1 - 5 for e-e length of pipe required. Use table of fitting sizes, Data #2, Appendix.

	c-c	Pipe	Ells	e-e
1.	18″	3/4″	90°	
2.	2′-1 1/2″	1/2″	90°	
3.	3′-4″	1″	90° and 45°	
4.	40″	1 1/4″	45°	
5.	5′-3″	1 1/2″	60°	

Unit 9 EQUAL SPACING

RELATED INFORMATION

In pipe fitting, equal spaces are equal c-c lengths.   Often the e-e lengths
are also equal, but not always.   Different e-e
lengths would result if the allowance for fitting
were not the same for each pipe.

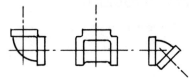

If one pipe assembly used a 90° ell and the
other a 45° ell, then the c-c lengths would be
alike. The e-e lengths, however, would differ
due to the difference in fitting allowance between
a 90° ell and a 45° ell.

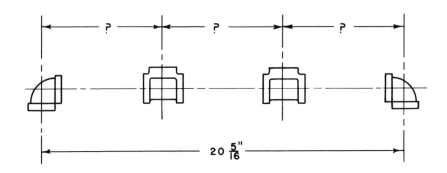

SAMPLE PROBLEM

Distance c-c is 20 5/16″. Divide into three equal spaces.

SOLUTION

Step 1: Convert to whole and decimal inches

20 5/16″ = 20.312″ (See Data #6, Appendix.)

Step 2: Divide

$$\begin{array}{r} 6.770 \\ 3\overline{)\,20.312} \end{array}$$

Step 3: Convert to nearest 16th inch.

6.77 becomes 6 3/4″   <u>Ans.</u>

ASSIGNMENT

In each of the following equal-spaced pipe problems, solve for c-c and e-e
lengths for each lettered pipe.

1.

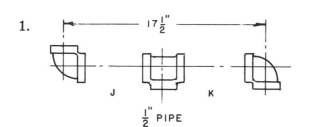

$17\frac{1}{2}$"

J   K

$\frac{1}{2}$" PIPE

	c-c	e-e
J		
K		

2.

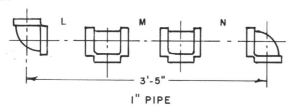

L   M   N

3'-5"

I" PIPE

	c-c	e-e
L		
M		
N		

3.

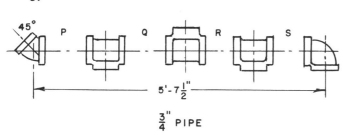

45°   P   Q   R   S

$5'-7\frac{1}{2}$"

$\frac{3}{4}$" PIPE

	c-c	e-e
P		
Q		
R		
S		

4.

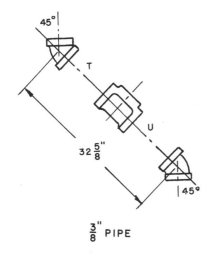

45°

T

U

$32\frac{5}{8}$"

45°

$\frac{3}{8}$" PIPE

	c-c	e-e
T		
U		

Unit 10   ANGLES IN PLUMBING

RELATED INFORMATION

The smaller sizes of pipe, under 1 1/4", have fittings available in 90° and 45° fitting angles. The larger sizes have fittings of 60°, 22 1/2° and 11 1/4°, as well as the 90° and 45° fittings.   In cast iron pipe, there is a 72° fitting, but no 11 1/4° fitting.

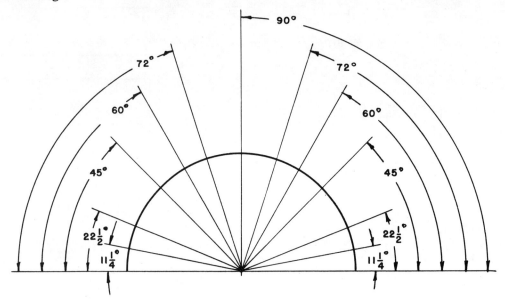

The fitting angle is measured between an extension of one center line to the other center line.   The larger the fitting angle, the greater the angle measure.

The complementary angle is often mistaken for the fitting angle. The complementary angle is found by subtracting the fitting angle from 90°.

$$C.A. = 90° - F.A.$$

$$C.A. = 90° - 60°$$

$$C.A. = 30°$$

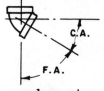

The larger the fitting angle, the smaller the complementary angle.

A bend is a fraction of a circle angle. The bend equals the fitting angle over 360°.

$$Bend = \frac{F.A.}{360°}$$

$$Bend = \frac{60°}{360°}$$

$$Bend = 1/6$$

A 1/6 bend is a cast iron elbow of 60° fitting angle. A 60° ell, or elbow is a threaded style fitting. The fitting angle equals the bend times 360°.

$$\text{F.A.} = \text{bend} \times 360°$$

$$\text{F.A.} = 1/6 \times 360°$$

$$\text{F.A.} = 60°$$

ASSIGNMENT

1. Complete the missing items in the following table:

F.A.	C.A.	Bend
90°		
72°		
60°	30°	1/6
45°		
22 1/2°		
11 1/4°		

2. If there were a 50° cast iron fitting, what bend would it be? _____

3. If there were a 1/9 bend, what fitting angle would it have? _____

    What complementary angle? _____

4. Write the plumbing trade name for each of the angles shown by letters in the following illustration.

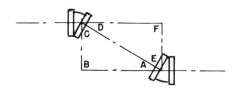

A _____

B _____

C _____

D _____

E _____

F _____

Unit 11   OFFSET, DIAGONAL, RISE OR RUN

RELATED INFORMATION
THE OFFSET

When two pipes are parallel to each other, they are an offset distance apart. They may both be horizontal or they may both be vertical, but A is parallel to B, (Fig. 1) and C is parallel to D, (Fig. 2). The distance between the center lines of the two parallel pipes is called offset. The offset is the center-to-center length if the parallel pipes are connected using 90° fittings (Fig. 3).

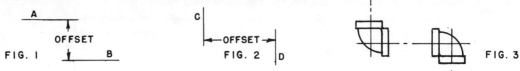

THE DIAGONAL

If two parallel pipes are connected by fittings other than 90° then the center-to-center length of the connecting pipe is a diagonal. The name comes from the diagonal of the square or rectangle as shown in Fig. 4. The diagonal construction is preferred to the 90° fittings because of less restriction to flow.

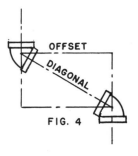

THE RISE OR RUN

Rise or run are the same distance. Figs. 5 and 6 show how the name changes. For parallel vertical pipes there is a rise. But for parallel horizontal pipes, there is a run. In some cases, run is referred to as "set" or even "setback".

SAMPLE PROBLEM

Make two pipe diagrams, one with pipes horizontal and the other with pipes vertical, using 60° fitting angles. Draw a rectangle around each pipe diagram and label each line with its plumbing trade name. Use a protractor to measure the fitting angles.

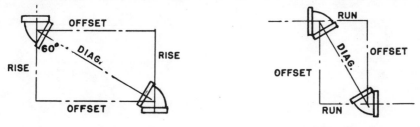

ASSIGNMENT

For each of the following fitting angles, construct two pipe diagrams, one with the diagonal connecting vertical pipes, the other with the diagonal connecting horizontal pipes. Enclose each diagonal with a square or rectangle and label each line.

1. 45° fitting angle

2. 22 1/2° fitting angle

3. 11 1/4° fitting angle

4. 72° fitting angle

Unit 12   SOLVING FOR 45° CONSTANTS

RELATED INFORMATION

The diagonal and offset are proportional. In other words, as illustrated by the sketch on the right, the offset and diagonal are dependent upon each other, and if one is changed, it produces a relative change in the other.

A ratio number called a constant represents this relative change. The diagonal multiplied by a certain constant equals the offset. The offset multiplied by a certain other constant equals the diagonal. For any given angle, these constants do not change.

It is quite simple to look up these constants on a data sheet. However, understanding how these constants were arrived at will help you understand how and why they are used. Only mathematics of a general nature is used but there are several steps.

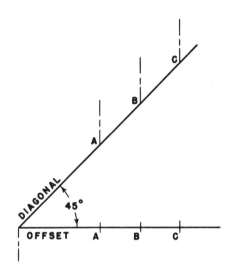

SAMPLE PROBLEM

Solve for the constants for a 45° diagonal, using an offset of 6″.

SOLUTION

1. Determine the run. Since the triangle formed by the run, offset, and diagonal has two equal angles, the sides must be equal.   Or, the sides of the square formed are equal. Thus, the run equals the offset, or 6″.

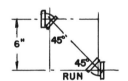

2. Solve for the diagonal. Diagonal = $\sqrt{\text{run}^2 + \text{offset}^2}$

    $= \sqrt{36 + 36}$ or $\sqrt{72}$

    $= 8.485$

3. Divide the diagonal by the offset. $8.485 \div 6 = 1.414$
   The diagonal, then, is 1.414 times as long as the offset. The offset multiplied by 1.414 = diagonal.

4. Divide the offset by the diagonal. $6 \div 8.485 = .707$
   The offset is .707 as long as the diagonal. The diagonal times .707 = offset.

30

ASSIGNMENT

1. Solve for the two constants as in the sample problem, using an offset of 9″.
    Show all your work.

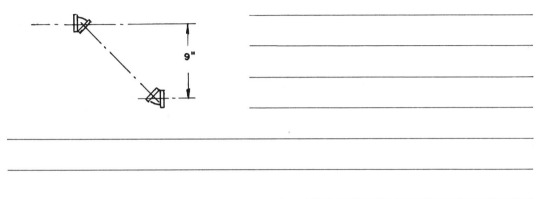

_____

_____

_____

_____

_____

_____

_____

_____

2. Assuming a 45° angle in each of the following, compute the missing infor-
    mation.

	Offset	Run	Diagonal
1.	10″		
2.		1′-4″	
3.			2′-6″
4.	3′-5″		
5.			3′-5″
6.	1′-2″		

Unit 13   45° DIAGONAL AND PIPE LENGTH

RELATED INFORMATION

A sequence of steps enables the plumber to determine the e-e length to cut the pipe to make up the diagonal.

The offset is measured from the job, but for problem purposes, it is given as a measured distance.

The diagonal is found by multiplying the offset by a constant; in this case, 1.414. This is the c-c or diagonal length.

The pipe length is found by making an allowance for fittings. Thus, this procedure can be used for any size or any kind of pipe.

SAMPLE PROBLEM

Compute the c-c and e-e length for pipe K.

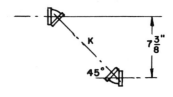

1" PIPE

1. Convert offset to decimal inches.

    7 3/8" = 7.375" (Data #6)

2. Multiply by constant.

    1.414 × 7.375 = 10.428250 or 10 7/16" (Data #6)

3. Make fitting allowance.

    45° ell, 1" pipe, C. F. = 1 1/8" (Data #2) × 2 (ells) = 2 1/4"

    Thread-in = 1/2" × 2 (thread-ins) = 1"

    2 1/4" - 1" = 1 1/4" subtracted from 10 7/16" = 9 3/16" e-e.

	c-c	e-e
K	10 7/16"	9 3/16"

32

ASSIGNMENT

For each offset and pipe size determine c-c and
e-e for pipe K.

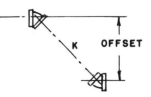

	Offset	Pipe Size	c-c	e-e
1.	8 1/4"	3/4"		
2.	9"	1"		
3.	11 1/2"	1/2"		
4.	18"	1 1/4"		
5.	22 3/4"	1 1/4"		
6.	24"	1 1/2"		
7.	2'-3 1/2"	1 1/2"		
8.	3'-9"	2"		
9.	5'-6 1/2"	2"		
10.	8'-2 1/4"	2 1/2"		

Unit 14   THREE-PIPE DIAGRAMS WITH 45° OFFSET

RELATED INFORMATION

The three-pipe diagram is often a part of a more complete pipe assembly. The methods of solving for diagonal length and of making the fittings allowance have been covered in previous units.

In this unit the rise is needed as a part of the solution for the third pipe. On the job, the plumber would measure overall, offset, and the c-c length for the first pipe. These dimensions are given in the problems.

SAMPLE PROBLEM

Solve for c-c and e-e dimensions of pipes J, K, and L as shown in the three-pipe diagram, using 45° offset.

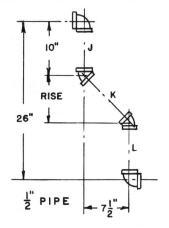

ANSWERS

	c-c	e-e
J	10"	9 1/8"
K	10 5/8"	10 1/8"
L	8 1/2"	7 5/8"

SOLUTION

1. Solve for pipe J. c-c is given as 10". Determine allowance for fittings (use Data #2).

One 90° ell, 1/2" pipe = -1 1/8"		= -1 7/8"	c-c of J	= 10"
One 45° ell, = - 3/4"			Fittings allowance	= - 7/8"
Two thread-ins (1/2" each)	= +1"		e-e of J	= 9 1/8"
Fittings allowance	= - 7/8"			Ans.

2. Solve for pipe K. Offset given as 7 1/2". Offset × 1.414 = c-c of K.

   7 1/2" = 7.5" × 1.414 = 10.6050" = 10 5/8" c-c of K   Ans.

34

Determine fittings allowance (Data #2).

Two 45° ells (3/4" each)	=	- 1 1/2"
Two thread-ins (1/2" each)	=	+ 1
Fitting allowance	=	- 1/2"

c-c of K	=	10 5/8"
Fitting allowance	=	- 1/2"
e-e of K	=	10 1/8"
		<u>Ans.</u>

3. Solve for pipe L.   Rise = offset in a 45° offset.   Rise = 7 1/2"

Overall - (c-c of J plus rise of K) = c-c of L
26" - (10" + 7 1/2") = 8 1/2" c-c of L   <u>Ans.</u>

L has same fittings as J (one 90° and one 45° ell) and same thread-ins so fitting allowances are the same.

8 1/2" - 7/8" = 7 5/8" e-e of L   <u>Ans.</u>

ASSIGNMENT

Solve for c-c and e-e dimensions for pipes J, K, and L of the three-pipe diagram shown. Use dimensions and pipe sizes given for each problem. Enter answers in the table supplied.

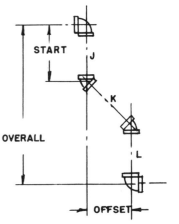

	Overall	Start	Offset	Pipe Size
1.	30"	9"	11"	1"
2.	42 1/2"	12"	13 1/2"	1/2"
3.	53 3/4"	15"	16"	3/4"
4.	60"	14"	32"	1 1/4"
5.	70"	Make J and L alike	34"	1 1/2"
6.	6'-0"	Make J and L alike	16 3/4"	1 1/2"

	J		K		L	
	c-c	e-e	c-c	e-e	c-c	e-e
1.						
2.						
3.						
4.						
5.						
6.						

Solve the following problems for c-c and e-e for pipes M, N, and O.

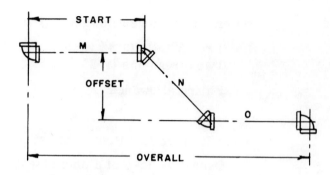

	Overall	Start	Offset	Pipe Size
7.	17″	5″	5 1/2″	3/8″
8.	33″	7 3/4″	8″	1/2″
9.	3′-3″	9 1/2″	9 1/2″	3/4″
10.	3′-9 3/4″	12 1/2″	15 1/2″	1″
11.	4′-0″	Make M and O alike	12″	1″
12.	4′-7″	Make M and O alike	21″	1 1/4″

	M		N		O	
	c-c	e-e	c-c	e-e	c-c	e-e
7.						
8.						
9.						
10.						
11.						
12.						

Unit 15   RIGHT ANGLE WITH 45° DIAGONAL

RELATED INFORMATION

Since two 45° fittings make 90°, it is common practice to use a 45° diagonal to make a right angle. As this can only be done with two 45° fittings, it is a special application. This 45° diagonal allows easier flow around the turn than a 90° ell as well as providing an alternate to avoid obstacles. Three on-the-job measurements are needed: the vertical overall, the horizontal overall and the start to the offset.

SAMPLE PROBLEM

Solve for c-c and e-e dimensions for pipes J, K, and L.

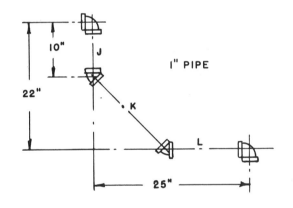

ANSWERS

	c-c	e-e
J	10″	8 5/8″
K	16 15/16″	15 15/16″
L	13″	11 5/8″

NOTE: Fitting allowance will hereafter be referred to as F. A.

1. Solve for pipe J. c-c is measured as 10″. Fittings allowance: one 90° ell, one 45° ell, two thread-ins (-1 3/8″, -1″, +1/2″, +1/2″) = -1 3/8″ F.A. 10″ - 1 3/8″ = 8 5/8″ e-e of J. <u>Ans.</u>

2. Solve for pipe K. Rise = offset. 22″ - 10″ = 12″ rise or 12″ offset. Offset × 1.414 = c-c of K. 12″ × 1.414 = 16.968″ = 16 15/16″ c-c of K. <u>Ans.</u>

    F.A. for K: two 45° ells, two thread-ins (-1″, -1″, +1/2″, +1/2″) = -1″ F.A. 16 15/16″ - 1″ = 15 15/16″ e-e of K. <u>Ans.</u>

3. Solve for pipe L. Run = offset = 12″. 25″ - 12″ = 13″ c-c of L. <u>Ans.</u>

    F.A. of L will be same as F.A. of J.   F.A. = -1 3/8″ 13″ - 1 3/8″ = 11 5/8″ e-e of J.   <u>Ans.</u>

ASSIGNMENT

Solve for c-c and e-e dimensions of pipes J, K, and L, using the dimensions listed in each numbered problem. Enter answers in the table supplied.

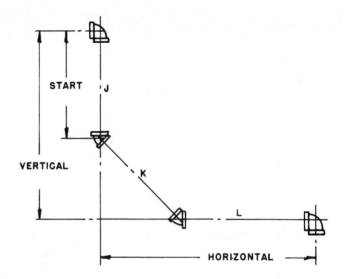

	Vertical	Horizontal	Start	Offset	Pipe
1.	30″	36″	16″		3/8″
2.	43″	38″	21″		2 1/2″
3.	4′	5′	1′-7 1/2″		2″
4.	5′-3″	4′-10″	2′-2 1/2″		1 1/4″
5.	6′-4″	5′-11″		3′-4 1/4″	3/4″

	J		K		L	
	c-c	e-e	c-c	e-e	c-c	e-e
1.						
2.						
3.						
4.						
5.						

Unit 16   45° OFFSET WITH WYE FITTING

RELATED INFORMATION

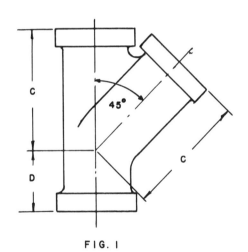

The 45° wye fitting could be used in a pipe diagram similar to the one in the previous unit. The plugged opening provides for a clean-out. The wye is also used to add a branch so that two fittings can waste into a single stack.

A study of Data #4, Appendix, and the following illustration, Fig. 1, shows that the center lines meet in such a way as to have two long centers and one short center for each wye.

This is different from ells which have equal centers, Fig. 2.

FIG. I

Nominal Pipe Size	C	D
$1 \frac{1}{2}''$	$3 \frac{5''}{16}$	$1 \frac{7''}{16}$
$2''$	$4 \frac{1''}{16}$	$1 \frac{13''}{16}$
$2'' \times 1 \frac{1}{2}''$	$4 \frac{1''}{4}$	$1 \frac{5''}{8}$
$2 \frac{1}{2}'' \times 2''$	$4 \frac{5''}{8}$	$1 \frac{5''}{8}$

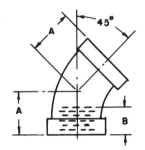

FIG. 2

In Figure 1, C represents the long center, D the short one. The excerpt from Data #4 shows the difference in these measurements for various sizes of wyes.

Dimension A in Figure 2 shows that the centers in elbows are equal.

39

SAMPLE PROBLEM

Solve for c-c and e-e lengths for pipes J, K, L, and M as shown in illustration below. (Use Data #2 for F.A.)

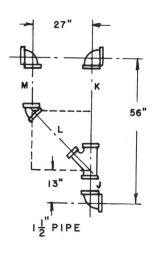

ANSWERS

	c-c	e-e
J	13"	10 11/16"
K	43"	38 13/16"
L	38 3/16"	34 3/8"
M	16"	13 5/8"

SOLUTION

Solve for pipe J.   c-c measures 13"

F.A. = - 1 7/8" (90° ell), - 1 7/16" (45° wye), + 1" (thread-ins)
F.A. = - 2 5/16"

13" - 2 5/16" = 10 11/16" e-e of J. Ans.

Solve for pipe K.   56" - 13" = 43" c-c of K. Ans.

F.A. = - 3 5/16"(long center of wye), - 1 7/8" (90° ell), + 1" (two thread-ins)
F.A. = - 4 3/16"

43" - 4 3/16" = 38 13/16" e-e of K. Ans.

Solve for pipe L. 27" (offset) × 1.414 = 38.178 = 38 3/16" c-c of L.   Ans.

F.A. = - 3 5/16" (long center of wye), - 1 1/2" (45° ell), + 1" (two thread-ins)
F.A. = - 3 13/16"

38 3/16" - 3 13/16" = 34 3/8" e-e of L. Ans.

Solve for pipe M.   offset (27") = rise.

56" - (13" + 27") = 16" c-c of M. Ans.

F.A. = - 1 1/2" (45° ell), - 1 7/8" (90° ell), + 1" (two thread-ins)
F.A. = - 2 3/8"
16" - 2 3/8" = 13 5/8" e-e of M. Ans.

ASSIGNMENT

Solve for c-c and e-e lengths for pipes J, K, L, and M in each of the following problems. Enter answers in the table supplied.

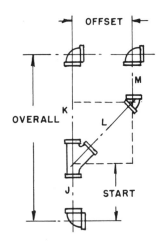

	Overall	Offset	Start	Pipe Size
1.	45 1/2″	23″	8″	1 1/2″
2.	5′-7″	2′-6″	15″	1 1/2″
3.	4′-5″	2′-0″	12″	2″
4.	4′-8″	9 3/4″	22″	2″
5.	26″	8 1/2″	11 3/4″	2″
6.	5′-10″	29″	19″	2″ (1 1/2″ branch)

	J		K		L		M	
	c-c	e-e	c-c	e-e	c-c	e-e	c-c	e-e
1.								
2.								
3.								
4.								
5.								
6.								

Unit 17   WYE AND TEE-WYE ASSEMBLIES

RELATED INFORMATION

The tee-wye is a 90° drainage fitting with an inside construction to cause as little turbulence as possible. Unlike a tee which has three equal centers (Fig. 1), the tee-wye has two long centers and one short center (Fig. 2).

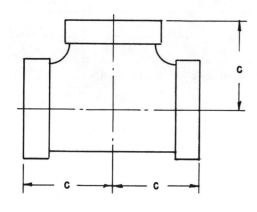

FIG. 1 TEE

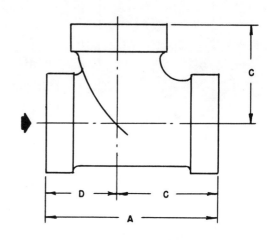

FIG. 2 TEE-WYE

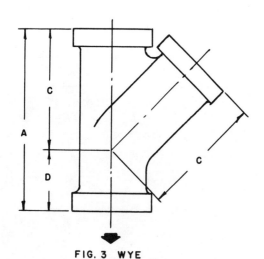

FIG. 3 WYE

Note that the flow is into the short center on the tee-wye (Fig. 2), while the flow is out of the short center on the wye (Fig. 3).

A IS FACE-TO-FACE
C IS CENTER-TO-FACE
D IS CENTER-TO-FACE (SHORT)

The wye and tee-wye fittings are used in various types of pipe assemblies with 45° diagonals.

42

SAMPLE PROBLEMS

1. Solve for c-c and e-e lengths of pipes J, K, L, and M shown in the following pipe diagram. (Assembly is similar to that of Unit 30 except for fitting allowance.)

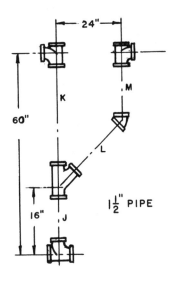

ANSWERS

	c-c	e-e
J	16″	13 1/16″
K	44″	39 3/16″
L	33 15/16″	30 1/8″
M	20″	17″

NOTE: Since the preceding units have covered in detail the procedures for finding fitting allowance (F.A.), solutions hereafter will simply list this information as plus or minus quantities.

SOLUTION

Solve for pipe J.
c-c measures 16″

$$
\begin{array}{ll}
\text{F.A.} = & -\ 2\ 1/2″ \\
 & -\ 1\ 7/16″ \\
 & +\ \ \ 1/2″ \\
 & +\ \ \ 1/2″ \\
\hline
\text{F.A.} = & -\ 2\ 15/16″
\end{array}
$$

e-e = 16″ - 2 15/16″ = 13 1/16″

Ans.

Pipe K.   60″ - 16″ = 44″ c-c   Ans.

$$
\begin{array}{ll}
\text{F.A.} = & -\ 3\ 5/16″ \\
 & -\ 2\ 1/2″ \\
 & +\ \ \ 1/2″ \\
 & +\ \ \ 1/2″ \\
\hline
\text{F.A.} = & -\ 4\ 13/16″
\end{array}
$$

e-e = 44″ - 4 13/16″ = 39 3/16″

Ans.

Pipe L.   24″ × 1.414 =
      33.936″ = 33 15/16″ c-c   Ans.

$$
\begin{array}{ll}
\text{F.A.} = & -\ 3\ 5/16″ \\
 & -\ 2\ 1/2″ \\
 & +\ \ \ 1/2″ \\
 & +\ \ \ 1/2″ \\
\hline
\text{F.A.} = & -\ 3\ 13/16″
\end{array}
$$

e-e = 33 15/16″ - 3 13/16″
e-e = 30 1/8″   Ans.

Pipe M.   60″ - (16″ + 24″) = 20″ c-c
                              Ans.

$$
\begin{array}{ll}
\text{F.A.} = & -\ 1\ 1/2″ \\
 & -\ 2\ 1/2″ \\
 & +\ \ \ 1/2″ \\
 & +\ \ \ 1/2″ \\
\hline
\text{F.A.} = & -\ 3″
\end{array}
$$

e-e = 20″ - 3″ = 17″   Ans.

2. Solve for c-c and e-e of pipes N, O, and P.

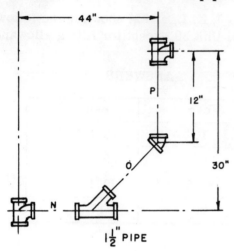

ANSWERS

	c-c	e-e
N	26″	23 1/16″
O	25 7/16″	21 5/8″
P	12″	9″

SOLUTION

Offset = 30″ - 12″ = 18″

Solve for pipe N.
44″ - 18″ = 26″ c-c

F.A. =	- 2 1/2″
	- 1 7/16″
	+ 1/2″
	+ 1/2″
F.A. =	- 2 15/16″

Solve for pipe O.
1.414 × 18 = 25.452 c-c

F.A. =	- 3 5/16″
	- 1 1/2″
	+ 1/2″
	+ 1/2″
F.A. =	- 3 13/16″

Solve for pipe P.

F.A. =	- 1 1/2″
	- 2 1/2″
	+ 1/2″
	+ 1/2″
F.A. =	- 3″

3. Solve for c-c and e-e of pipe Q. (Procedures for other pipes are covered in previous problems)

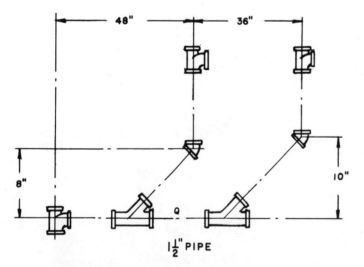

ANSWERS

	c-c	e-e
Q	34″	30 1/4″

SOLUTION

F.A. =	- 3 5/16″
	- 1 7/16″
	+ 1/2″
	+ 1/2″
F.A. =	- 3 3/4″

36″ - 10″ = 26″
(Note subtraction of outside run)

26″ + 8″ = 34″ c-c of Q.
(Note addition of inside run)

ASSIGNMENT

Solve for c-c and e-e of each pipe, using dimensions as given for each problem. Enter answers in the tables supplied.

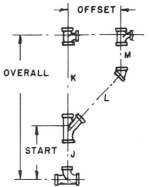

	Overall	Start	Offset	Pipe Size
1.	62″	14″	27″	1 1/2″
2.	5′-10″	19 1/2″	2′-7″	1 1/2″
3.	6′-5 1/2″	21 3/4″	2′-9 1/2″	2″
4.	7′-4″	2′-3″	3′-1 1/4″	2″
5.	9′-1 1/2″	2′-10 1/2″	3′-7″	2″ (1 1/2″ branch)

	J		K		L		M	
	c-c	e-e	c-c	e-e	c-c	e-e	c-c	e-e
1.								
2.								
3.								
4.								
5.								

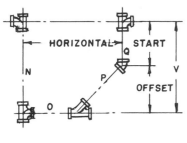

	Horizontal	Vertical	Start	Offset	Pipe Size
6.	40″	50″	30″		1 1/2″
7.	46″	32″		12 1/2″	1 1/2″
8.	3′-7 3/4″	5′-3″	2′-11″		2″
9.	5′-1 1/2″	4′-10 1/4″		2′-5″	2″
10.	3′-2″	4′-1 1/2″	1′-9 1/2″		2″ (1 1/2″ branch)

	N		O		P		Q	
	c-c	e-e	c-c	e-e	c-c	e-e	c-c	e-e
6.								
7.								
8.								
9.								
10.								

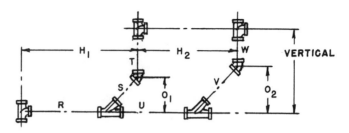

	H₁	H₂	Vertical	O₁	O₂	Pipe Size
11.	38″	25″	40″	8″	8″	1 1/2″
12.	42″	31″	53″	12″	9″	1 1/2″
13.	3′-7 1/2″	2′-4″	4′-10 1/2″	10″	10″	2″
14.	3′-9″	2′-5 3/4″	5′-0″	1′-2″	1′-7″	2″
15.	4′-7 3/4″	3′-5″	6′-2 1/2″	1′-5 1/2″	1′-9″	2″

		11.	12.	13.	14.	15.
R	c-c					
	e-e					
S	c-c					
	e-e					
T	c-c					
	e-e					
U	c-c					
	e-e					
V	c-c					
	e-e					
W	c-c					
	e-e					

16. This is an assembly for under the floor instead of in the wall. Solve for c-c and e-e lengths of pipes A, B, C, D, and E.

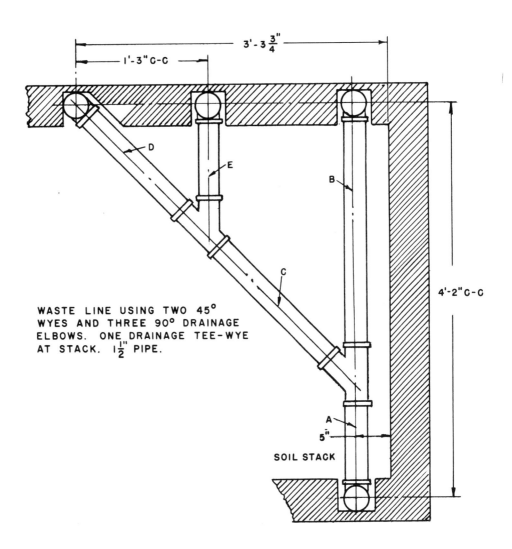

WASTE LINE USING TWO 45°
WYES AND THREE 90° DRAINAGE
ELBOWS. ONE DRAINAGE TEE-WYE
AT STACK. $1\frac{1}{2}$" PIPE.

SOIL STACK

	c-c	e-e
A		
B		
C		
D		
E		

Unit 18   THE .707 CONSTANT IN 45° PIPE ASSEMBLIES

RELATED INFORMATION

The use of a 45° ell and a wye to turn a corner works equally well with any diagonal length. The pipe fitter can use a stock nipple or other threaded pipe length to make up the diagonal. It is then necessary to determine the c-c or diagonal length and the offset or run.

In preceding units, we have been finding the c-c length by first finding the offset and multiplying by 1.414. Now we find the diagonal or c-c length and multiply it by .707 to find the offset. The rise (or run) length for 45° diagonals is equal to the offset.

SAMPLE PROBLEM

Solve for c-c and e-e lengths of pipes J, K, and L.

ANSWERS

	c-c	e-e
J	8″	6″
K	10 3/8″	8″
L	15 3/8″	13″

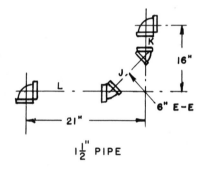

$1\frac{1}{2}$″ PIPE

SOLUTION

Pipe J.   e-e measures 6″

F.A. =
- 1 1/2″
- 1 1/2″
+ 1/2″
+ 1/2″

F.A. =   - 2″

c-c = 6″ + 2″ = 8″

(Note: c-c must be larger than
e-e so the F.A. is added)

Pipe K.   Offset = diagonal × .707

Offset = 8″ × .707 = 5.656 = 5 5/8″
(also run)

16″ - 5 5/8″ = 10 3/8″ = c-c of K.

F.A. =
- 1 1/2″
- 1 7/8″
+ 1/2″
+ 1/2″

F.A. =   - 2 3/4″

e-e = 10 3/8″ - 2 3/8″ = 8″
(Here, we subtract from the c-c to
get the smaller e-e length)

Pipe L.   21″ - 5 5/8″ = 15 3/8″ c-c
F.A. = - 1 1/2″, - 1 7/8″, + 1/2″, + 1/2″ = - 2 3/8″
15 3/8″ - 2 3/8″ = 13″ e-e of L.

ASSIGNMENT

Solve for c-c and e-e lengths for each lettered pipe in the following diagrams and find the offset for each diagram.

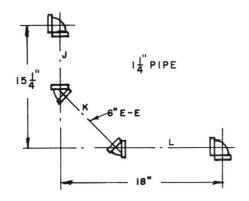

	c-c	e-e
J		
K		
L		
Offset		

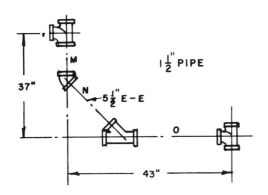

	c-c	e-e
M		
N		
O		
Offset		

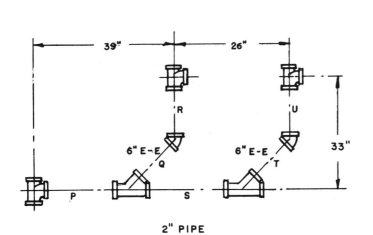

2" PIPE

	c-c	e-e
P		
Q		
R		
S		
T		
U		
Offset		

Unit 19   TO SOLVE FOR 60° CONSTANTS

RELATED INFORMATION

It is not too difficult to solve for the constants of a 60° offset. It gives the plumber added confidence to know that they are found with the aid of average mathematical knowledge.

SAMPLE PROBLEM

Solve for constants for diagonal from offset and rise using a triangle with 60° angles.

1. Take any equilateral triangle. In this case, we shall use one with 6″ sides.

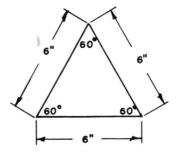

2. Cut this triangle with a line from the vertex and perpendicular to the base, line A-A.

3. Solve for the altitude (a) or offset.

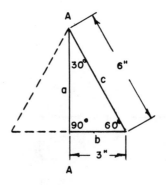

$$a = \sqrt{c^2 - b^2}$$

$$= \sqrt{36 - 9}$$

$$= \sqrt{27}$$

$$a = 5.196''$$

4. Divide the diagonal, 6″, by offset, 5.196″.

$$5.196 \overline{)6.000} = 1.154$$

The diagonal, then, is 1.154 times as long as the offset.

5. Divide the run, 3″, by the offset, 5.196″.

$$5.196 \overline{)3.000} = .577 \quad \text{The run is .577 times as long as the offset.}$$

50

ASSIGNMENT

1. Why are the constants true for any 60° offset?_____

    _____

    _____

2. The diagonal is how many times as long as the run? _____

3. The run is how many times as long as the diagonal? _____

4. The offset is how many times as long as the diagonal? _____

5. Why is the third angle 30°?_____

    _____

6. Why was the base of the equilateral triangle cut in equal parts by a line

    from the vertex perpendicular to the base?_____

    _____

    _____

Unit 20   SOLUTIONS WITH 60° DIAGONALS

RELATED INFORMATION

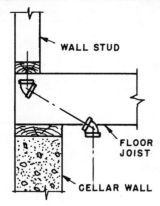

The 60° offset enables the pipe fitter to conceal pipe in walls or miss obstructions when the usual 45° diagonal will not do. The 60° angle gives a large offset for a smaller rise (or run).

Since the rise and offset are not equal there is an additional step needed to determine the rise. The use of a protractor avoids confusion between rise and offset lines. The 60° fittings are available for 1 1/4″ pipe and larger.

SAMPLE PROBLEM

Solve for c-c and e-e lengths of pipes J, K, and L.

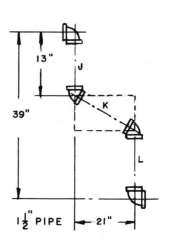

ANSWERS

	c-c	e-e
J	13″	10 3/8″
K	24 1/4″	21 3/4″
L	13 7/8″	11 1/4″

SOLUTION

Determine length of diagonal (c-c of K).   Offset × 1.154
21 × 1.154 = 24.234 = 24 1/4″ c-c of K.

Determine rise.   Offset × .577   21 × .577 = 12.117 or 12 1/8″

Check by doubling the rise. It should equal the diagonal.
12.117 × 2 = 24.234 = diagonal

Solve for pipe J.
c-c given as 13″
F.A. = - 1 7/8″
        - 1 3/4″
        +   1/2″
        +   1/2″
        _____
F.A. = - 2 5/8″
13″ - 2 5/8″ =
    10 3/8″ e-e

Solve for pipe K.

F.A. = - 1 3/4″
        - 1 3/4″
        +   1/2″
        +   1/2″
        _____
F.A. = - 2 1/2″

24 1/4″ - 2 1/2″ =
    21 3/4″ e-e

Solve for pipe L.
39″ - (13″ + 12 1/8″ rise)
    = 13 7/8″ c-c

F.A. = - 2 5/8″
        (same as J)

13 7/8″ - 2 5/8″ =
    11 1/4″ e-e

52

ASSIGNMENT

Solve for c-c and e-e lengths for each lettered pipe in the following problems.

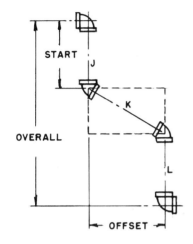

	Overall	Offset	Start	Pipe Size
1.	46″	23″	15″	1 1/4″
2.	72″	35 1/2″	27″	1 1/4″
3.	4′-7″	2′-2″	10″	1 1/2″
4.	10′-6″	4′-5″	2′-6 1/2″	2″
5.	3′-9 1/2″	24″	16″	2 1/2″

	J c-c	J e-e	K c-c	K e-e	L c-c	L e-e
1.						
2.						
3.						
4.						
5.						

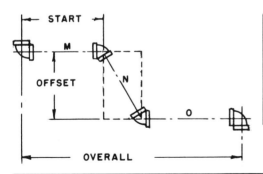

	Overall	Offset	Start	Pipe Size
6.	30″	15″	6″	1 1/4″
7.	62″	33″	20″	1 1/2″
8.	10′-7″	4′-3″	4′-3″	2″

	M c-c	M e-e	N c-c	N e-e	O c-c	O e-e
6.						
7.						
8.						

9. Solve for c-c and e-e dimensions for each lettered pipe in the diagram
   below.

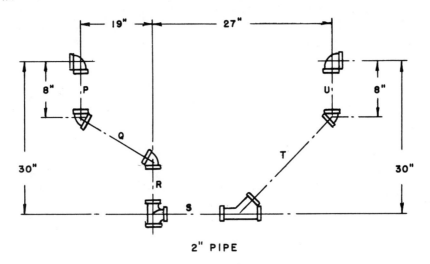

2" PIPE

	c-c	e-e
P		
Q		
R		
S		
T		
U		

Unit 21 SOLUTIONS WITH 22 1/2° DIAGONALS

RELATED INFORMATION

The 22 1/2° fitting gives a long diagonal and rise for a small offset. Thus it is the opposite of a 60° offset. The 22 1/2° fitting can be used where an offset is required in a limited space.

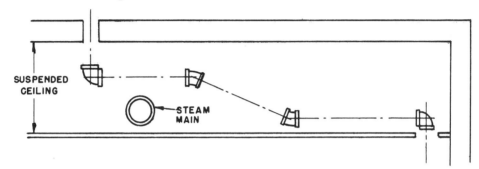

Since the angle is different it follows that different constants are used from other offsets. These constants are not readily solved for but can be found in Data #9, which has been compiled in the Appendix of this book.

SAMPLE PROBLEM

Solve for c-c and e-e length of pipes J, K, and L. (Note: Unit 20 and preceding units have presented detailed solutions of c-c, F.A. and e-e dimensions. These steps will now be abbreviated with only the essential figures listed in the solutions.)

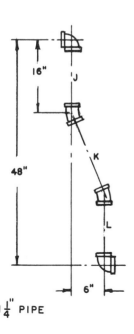

ANSWERS

	c-c	e-e
J	16″	14 1/8″
K	15 11/16″	14 7/16″
L	17 1/2″	15 5/8″

SOLUTION

Diagonal: $2.613 \times 6″ = 15.678$ Rise: $2.414 \times 6″ = 14.484$

Pipe J and L	Pipe K	Pipe L	
- 1 3/4″	- 1 1/8″	16″	48″
- 1 1/8″	- 1 1/8″	+ 14 1/2	- 30 1/2
+ 1/2″	+ 1/2″	30 1/2″	17 1/2″
+ 1/2″	+ 1/2″		c-c
- 1 7/8″ F.A.	- 1 1/4″ F.A.		

55

ASSIGNMENT

Solve for c-c and e-e length of each lettered pipe in the following problems.

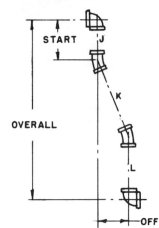

	Overall	Start	Offset	Pipe Size
1.	52″	14″	7″	1 1/4″
2.	26 1/2″	9″	3 1/2″	1 1/2″
3.	4′-11″	1′-5″	9″	2″
4.	6′-5″	1′-8 3/4″	1′-6″	2 1/2″

	J		K		L	
	c-c	e-e	c-c	e-e	c-c	e-e
1.						
2.						
3.						
4.						

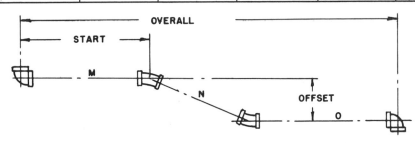

	Overall	Start	Offset	Pipe Size
5.	33″	11″	3 1/4″	1 1/2″
6.	70″	20″	13″	2″
7.	7′-9″	2′-1″	2′-2″	2 1/2″

	M		N		O	
	c-c	e-e	c-c	e-e	c-c	e-e
5.						
6.						
7.						

8. Solve for c-c and e-e dimensions of all pipes shown in the following diagram. Use dimensions as given on the drawing.

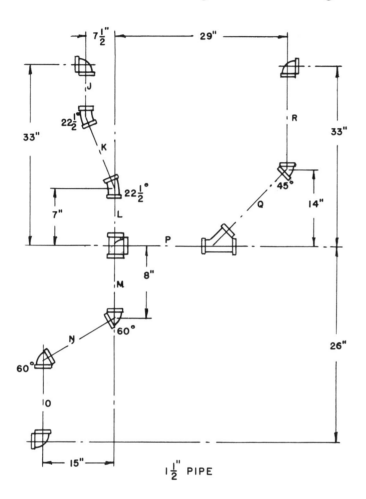

	c-c	e-e
J		
K		
L		
M		
N		
O		
P		
Q		
R		

Unit 22   SOLUTIONS WITH 11 1/4° DIAGONALS

RELATED INFORMATION

The 11 1/4° diagonal is more than five times as long as the offset. Thus, the offset can be an inch or less and the diagonal length provides room for fittings and a nipple. As 1 1/4″ and larger pipe is very rigid, there is need for fittings to make small offsets. The 11 1/4° fittings provide the pipefitter with another possibility in installing pipe to bypass.obstructions met on the job.

SAMPLE PROBLEM

Solve for c-c and e-e lengths of pipes J, K, and L.

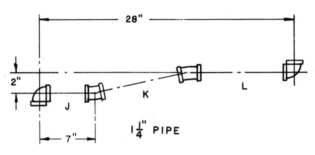

ANSWERS

	c-c	e-e
J	7″	5 1/4″
K	10 1/4″	9 1/4″
L	10 15/16″	9 3/16″

SOLUTION

Diagonal: 5.126 × 2″ = 10.252″ or 10 1/4″

Run: 5.027 × 2″ = 10.054″ or 10 1/16″

Pipe J and L	Pipe K	Pipe L	
- 1 3/4″	- 1″	7″	28″
- 1″	- 1″	+ 10 1/16″	- 17 1/16″
+ 1/2″	+ 1/2″	17 1/16″	10 15/16″ c-c
+ 1/2″	+ 1/2″		
- 1 3/4″	- 1″		

ASSIGNMENT

Solve for c-c and e-e of each lettered pipe in the following problems.

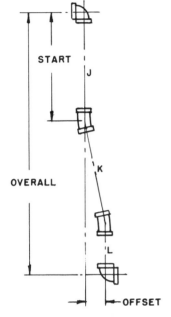

	Overall	Start	Offset	Pipe Size
1.	52″	14″	5 1/2″	1 1/4″
2.	80″	22″	7″	1 1/2″
3.	6′-9 1/2″	3′-7″	3″	2″
4.	9′-3″	4′-0″	1 1/4″	2 1/2″

	J		K		L	
	c-c	e-e	c-c	e-e	c-c	e-e
1.						
2.						
3.						
4.						

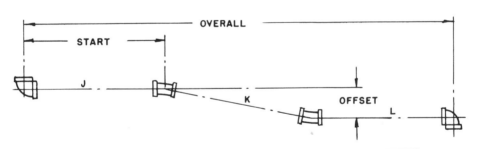

	Overall	Start	Offset	Pipe Size
5.	67″	10″	8″	1 1/2″
6.	5′-7″	1′-5″	4 1/2″	2″
7.	7′-3″	2′-4 1/2″	2 1/2″	2 1/2″

	J		K		L	
	c-c	e-e	c-c	e-e	c-c	e-e
5.						
6.						
7.						

8. Solve for c-c and e-e lengths of the lettered pipes shown in the following diagram. Use dimensions as shown.

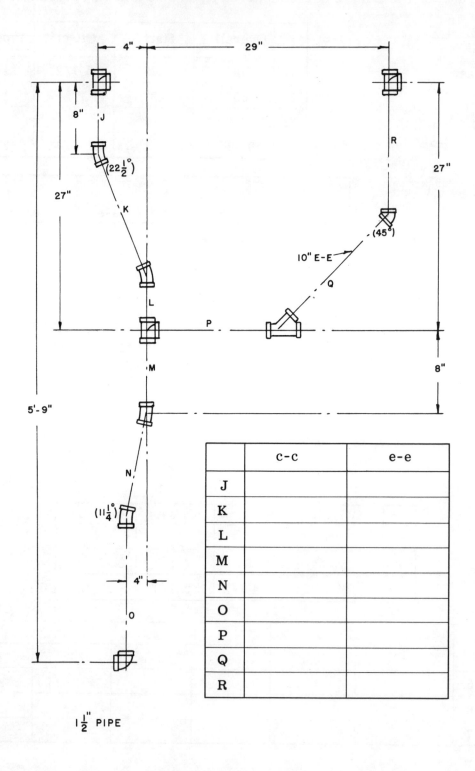

	c-c	e-e
J		
K		
L		
M		
N		
O		
P		
Q		
R		

$1\frac{1}{2}"$ PIPE

9. Two parallel pipes are offset as shown in the diagram below. The pipe size is 1 1/2" so all of the threaded ells are available. Choose an angle for the diagonal so that the pipe can be installed in the space shown. Compute the diagonal and the rise.

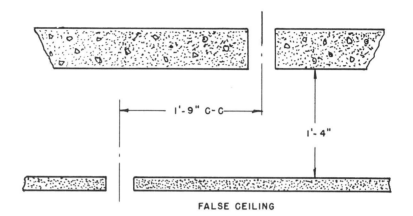

FALSE CEILING

Diagonal angle _____

Diagonal length _____

Rise   _____

Unit 23   CAST IRON PIPE

RELATED INFORMATION

Cast iron pipe is very durable in most cases and is preferred to wrought iron or steel pipe where long service with little maintenance is expected. Connections are made by one of the three methods shown in the half-section views. The lead and oakum joint can be used either with beaded or plain spigot end pipe. The compression gasket uses plain spigot end pipe. The No-Hub connection is available for 2″, 3″, and 4″ cast iron pipe and fittings. The outside diameter of No-Hub pipe is a little smaller than the outside diameter of extra-heavy cast iron pipe.

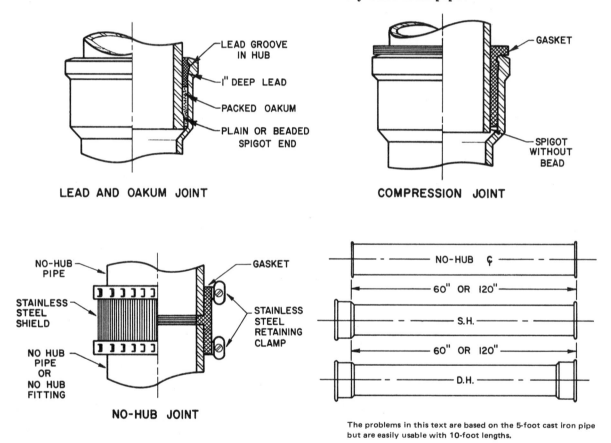

LEAD AND OAKUM JOINT

COMPRESSION JOINT

NO-HUB JOINT

The problems in this text are based on the 5-foot cast iron pipe but are easily usable with 10-foot lengths.

Pipe is cast in 5-foot and 10-foot lengths. For No-Hub pipe this is the actual, or laying, pipe length. Single hub pipe has a laying length of 5 or 10 feet; this is the pipe length without measuring the hub. Any part cut off a single hub length has no hub. Such "bald" pieces are often scrap and are as short as planning can allow. The double hub piece can be a saving as it will make two shorter pieces each with a hub. The laying length of double hub pipe is shorter than 60 inches or 120 inches by one hub depth. The laying length for 4″ D.H.C.I. is 57 inches for 5-foot pipe and 117 inches for 10-foot pipe. The overall lengths (of single and double hub pipe) are alike, probably as an aid to the molding and casting of pipe.

SAMPLE PROBLEMS

1. How many full lengths and how long an additional piece are needed for a cast iron line, 16'-2" e-e?

$$
\begin{array}{l}
16'\text{-}2'' \\
\underline{-\ 15'\text{-}0''}\ \ (5' \times 3) \\
\ \ \ 1'\text{-}2'' \qquad \text{3 full lengths and a 1'-2" piece} \quad \underline{\text{Ans.}}
\end{array}
$$

2. (a) How much is left after cutting 1'-2" from a single hub pipe?

    (b) From a double hub pipe with a 3" deep hub?

(a) 5'-0" = 60"	(b) 5'-0" = 60"	57"
$\underline{-\ 14''}$	60" - 3" = 57"	$\underline{-\ 14''}$
46" Ans.	1'-2" = 14"	43" Ans.

ASSIGNMENT

For each length given determine:

a. Number of cast iron single hub pipe needed.

b. Length of any piece less than a full pipe.

c. How much is left after cutting the piece from an S. H. pipe.

d. How much is left after cutting the piece from a D. H. pipe with 3" hub depth.

	Total Length	a. No. of Full S.H. Lengths	b. Length of Piece	c. Remainder if Piece is cut from S.H.	d. Remainder if Piece is cut from D.H.
1.	10'-10"	2	10"	50"	47"
2.	13'-7"				
3.	22'-5"				
4.	49'-2"				
5.	63'-8"				

Unit 24   LEAD AND OAKUM FOR CAST IRON JOINT

RELATED INFORMATION

The plumbing code (Buffalo, N. Y.*) specifies a minimum of 12 ounces of fine soft lead per inch of diameter of pipe for pouring a hub to join cast iron pipe. As the smallest cast iron pipe is 2″ size, it requires 2 × 12 ounces or 24 ounces of lead for one 2″ pipe joint.

The specified amount of oakum is 2 ounces per inch of diameter. Thus a 2″ pipe hub would require 4 ounces of oakum. The estimator could, at his judgment, expect somewhat larger amounts of lead because of spillage and overpouring. The problems of this book are based on the code requirements although estimating practice generally specifies 1 pound of lead for each inch of diameter of pipe.

> * If your local code differs from the figures described in this unit, it is advisable to insert your local code requirements.

SAMPLE PROBLEM

How much lead would be required to pour five joints for 3″ pipe? How much oakum?

SOLUTION

Joints   Code   Size

$5 \times 12 \times 3 = 180$ ounces or $\dfrac{180}{16} = 11\ 1/4$ lbs. lead <u>Ans.</u>

$5 \times 2 \times 3 = 30$ ounces or $\dfrac{30}{16} = 1$ lb. 14 oz. oakum <u>Ans.</u>

ASSIGNMENT

1. Complete the table for lead and oakum per joint.

Pipe Size	Lead		Oakum	
	Ounces	Pounds	Ounces	Pounds
1″ code	12	3/4	2	1/8
2″ code				
3″ code				
4″ code				
5″ code				
6″ code				

Unit 25   CAST IRON ASSEMBLIES WITH 1/4 BENDS

RELATED INFORMATION

The cast iron fitting that is used similarly to a threaded ell is called a "bend". A 1/4 bend is a quarter of a circle, thus a 90° fitting. A bend has a long center and a short center. In data the long center is shown as "D", the short center as "C".

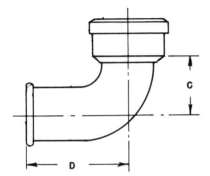

The long center, D, is measured to the spigot end, but the short center, C, is measured to the bottom of the hub. There has to be a hub on the bend but it is not included in the short center length. The corner of the hub on the outside very nearly corresponds to the hub depth on the inside so that hub fittings are easy to measure to the bottom of the hub.

Calculations for cast iron assemblies should include planning to use single hub and double hub pipe economically as well as estimating the pounds of lead required. Oakum could also be estimated but the plumber finds that a supply of oakum is easy to have on hand.

SAMPLE PROBLEM

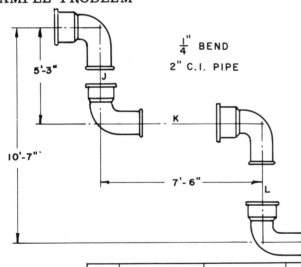

a. Solve for c-c and e-e lengths of pipes J, K, and L.

b. Determine the number of S.H. and D.H. pipes needed.

c. Estimate lbs. of lead to assemble but not to connect to other piping.

F.A. of J, K, and L

(See Data #12, Appendix)

$$\begin{array}{r} - 6'' \\ - 3\ 1/4'' \\ \hline - 9\ 1/4''\ \text{F.A.} \end{array}$$

	c-c	e-e	C.I. Pipe Required
J	63"	53 3/4"	1 S.H.
K	90"	80 3/4"	1 S.H. + 20 3/4" from D.H.
L	64"	54 3/4"	1 S.H.
C.I. Pipe to Order			3 S.H. and 1 D.H.

c. 7 hubs to pour. $7 \times 12/16 \times 2 = 163/16 = 10\ 1/2$ lbs. lead

65

ASSIGNMENT

a. Solve for c-c and e-e lengths of each pipe in the diagram.

b. Make a list of single hub and double hub lengths needed.

c. Compute the pounds of lead to pour the hubs.

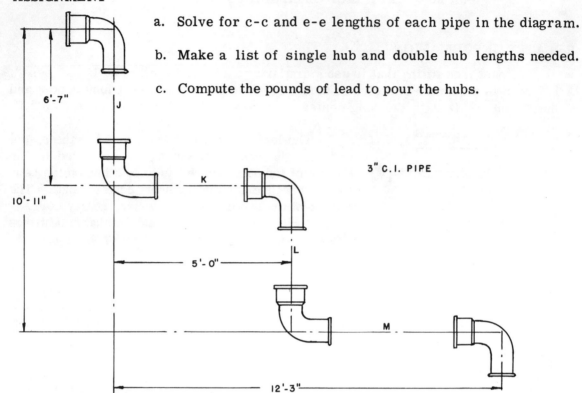

	a.		b.
	c-c	e-e	C. I. Pipe Required
J			
K			
L			
M			
Lbs. Lead Required			

Unit 26 CAST IRON ASSEMBLIES WITH VARIOUS BENDS

RELATED INFORMATION

The center-to-center lengths for cast iron assemblies are the same as for threaded pipe. It is the allowance for fittings that is somewhat different. It is necessary to become accustomed that a 1/6 bend is 60°, a 1/8 bend is 45°, and a 1/16 bend is 22 1/2°. Since these angles are the same as for threaded fittings, it follows that the same corresponding constants are used.

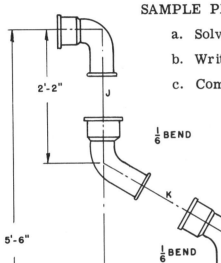

SAMPLE PROBLEM

a. Solve for c-c and e-e lengths of pipes J, K, and L.

b. Write order for fittings and pipe required.

c. Compute pounds of lead required.

SOLUTION (Note: Use Data #14)

Diagonal = $36'' \times 1.154 = 41.544 = 41\ 9/16''$

Rise = $36'' \times .577 = 20.772 = 20\ 3/4''$

ANSWERS

	c-c	e-e
J	2'-2"	1'-6"
K	3'-5 9/16"	2'-10 13/16"
L	1'-7 1/4"	11 1/4"

a. Pipe J - 6"   26"
           - 2"   - 8"
           - 8" F.A.   18" = 1'-6" e-e

     Pipe K - 4 3/4"   41 9/16"
               - 2   - 6 3/4"
               - 6 3/4" F.A.   34 13/16" e-e

Pipe L   26" + 20 3/4" = 46 3/4"   - 4 3/4"   19 1/4"
               66" - 46 3/4" = 19 1/4" c-c   - 3 1/4"   - 8
                                              - 8" F.A.   11 1/4" e-e

Cut J and K from a D.H. piece
Cut L from a D.H. and save remainder

b.

	Bill of Material
2	2", 1/4 Bends XHCI
2	2", 1/6 Bends XHCI
2	2", D.H. XHCI

c. 6 joints = $\dfrac{6 \times 2 \times 12}{16}$ = 9 lbs. lead

67

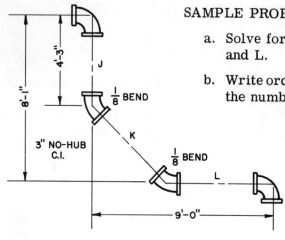

Pipe J Pipe K Pipe L

-5″   -3″   -3″

-3″   -3″   -5″

‾‾‾‾   ‾‾‾‾   ‾‾‾‾

-8″   -6″   -8″

SAMPLE PROBLEM #2

a. Solve for c-c and e-e length of No-Hub pipes J, K, and L.

b. Write order for fittings and pipe required. Include the number of connectors.

SOLUTION (Note: Use Data #28)

a. Offset = 8′-1″ – 4′-3″ = 3′-10″
Run = Offset = 3′-10″
Diagonal = 46″ × 1.414 = 65.044″
L = 9′-0″ = 3′-10″ = 5′-2″

ANSWERS

	c-c	e-e
J	4′ - 3″	3′-7″
K	5′-5 1/16″	4′-11 1/16″
L	5′-2″	4′-6″

b.

	Bill of Material
2	3″, 1/4 Bends, No-Hub
2	3″, 1/8″ Bends, No-Hub
3	3″, 5′ C.I., No-Hub
6	3″, Connectors, No-Hub

ASSIGNMENT

For each problem which follows:

a. Solve for c-c and e-e lengths. (The problems may also be used for No-Hub pipe. Use Data No. 28.)

b. Write an order list for fittings and pipe.

c. Compute the pounds of lead or number of No-Hub connections required.

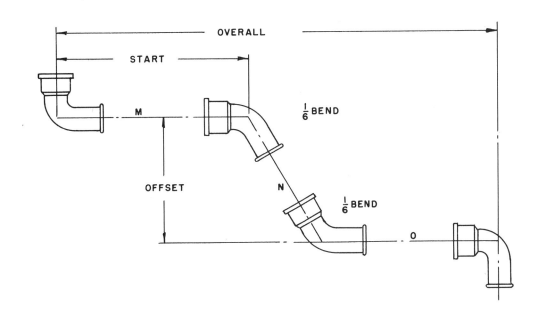

	Overall	Start	Offset	Pipe Size
1	60″	22″	18″	2″
2	8′-0″	2′-0″	4′-0″	3″
3	3′-10″	1′-3″	1′-4″	3″
4	14′-6″	7′-0″	2′-9″	4″

	M			N			O		
	c-c	e-e	No-Hub e-e	c-c	e-e	No-Hub e-e	c-c	e-e	No-Hub e-e
1									
2									
3									
4									

	Pipe	No-Hub Pipe	Pounds of Lead	No-Hub Connectors
1				
2				
3				
4				

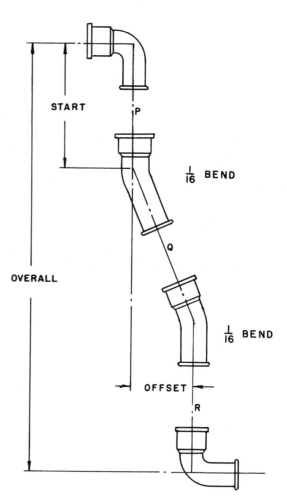

	Over-all	Start	Offset	Pipe Size
5	5'-5"	20"	7"	2"
6	70"	24"	10 1/2"	3"
7	7'-8"	2'-6"	1'-0"	4"
8	12'-9"	5'-2"	1'-9"	4"

	P			Q			R		
	c-c	e-e	No-Hub e-e	c-c	e-e	No-Hub e-e	c-c	e-e	No-Hub e-e
5									
6									
7									
8									

	Pipe	No-Hub Pipe	Pounds of Lead	No-Hub Connectors
5				
6				
7				
8				

Unit 27   1/5 BEND OFFSETS

RELATED INFORMATION

Cast iron bends are made with a 72° fitting angle.   These are 1/5 bends (360° ÷ 5 = 72°). There is no similar fitting angle in threaded fittings.

It may be well to notice that the 11 1/4° fitting angle available in threaded fittings is not available in cast iron. Thus, each style of fittings has one angle not available to both kinds of pipe.

It is, of course, necessary to use a new set of constants to work with 1/5 bends. They are given in Data #11, Appendix.

SAMPLE PROBLEMS

1. Solve for c-c and e-e lengths of pipes J, K, and L.

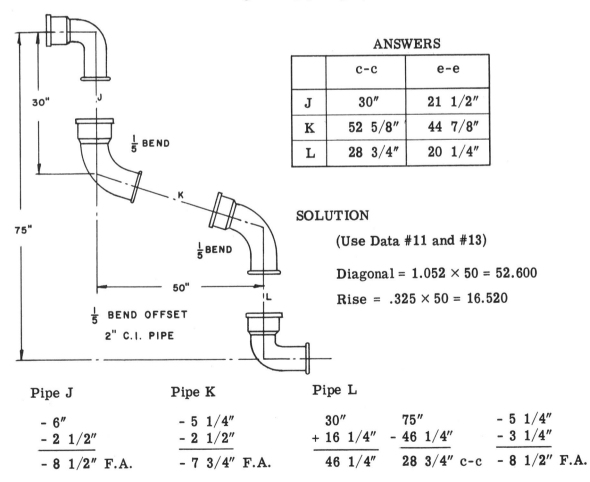

ANSWERS

	c-c	e-e
J	30″	21 1/2″
K	52 5/8″	44 7/8″
L	28 3/4″	20 1/4″

SOLUTION

(Use Data #11 and #13)

Diagonal = 1.052 × 50 = 52.600

Rise = .325 × 50 = 16.520

Pipe J	Pipe K	Pipe L		
- 6″	- 5 1/4″	30″	75″	- 5 1/4″
- 2 1/2″	- 2 1/2″	+ 16 1/4″	- 46 1/4″	- 3 1/4″
- 8 1/2″ F.A.	- 7 3/4″ F.A.	46 1/4″	28 3/4″ c-c	- 8 1/2″ F.A.

71

2. What is the shortest diagonal that can be made with two, 2″, 1/5 bends? What is the offset?   What is the rise?

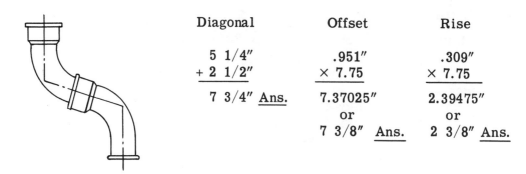

Diagonal	Offset	Rise
5 1/4″	.951″	.309″
+ 2 1/2″	× 7.75	× 7.75
7 3/4″ Ans.	7.37025″	2.39475″
	or	or
	7 3/8″ Ans.	2 3/8″ Ans.

ASSIGNMENT

a. Solve for c-c and e-e for each lettered pipe.

b. Write an order list for each assembly.

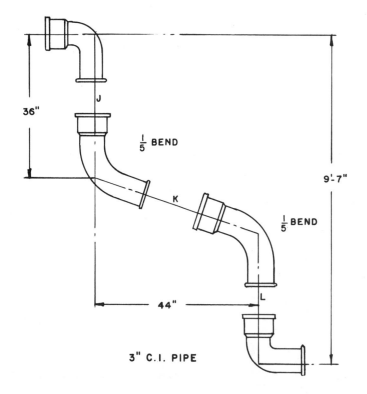

ANSWERS

	c-c	e-e
J		
K		
L		

	Bill of Materials

	c-c	e-e
M		
N		
O		

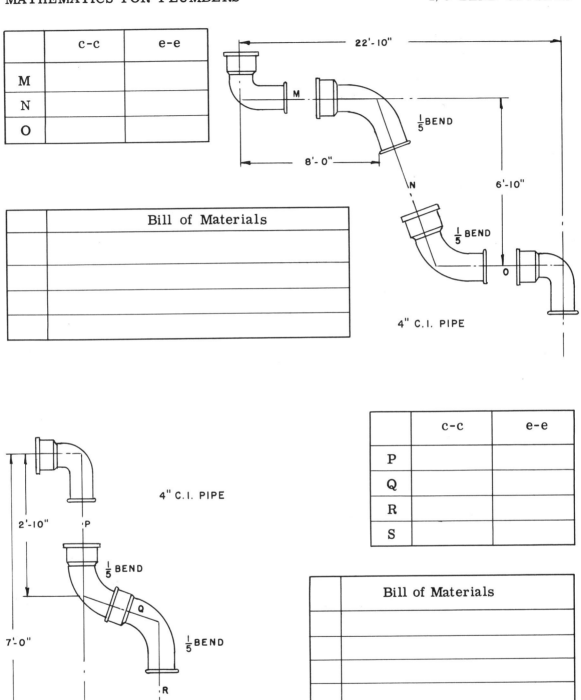

22'-10"

M

$\frac{1}{5}$ BEND

8'-0"

N

6'-10"

$\frac{1}{5}$ BEND

O

4" C.I. PIPE

	Bill of Materials		

4" C.I. PIPE

2'-10"

P

$\frac{1}{5}$ BEND

Q

$\frac{1}{5}$ BEND

7'-0"

R

S

3'-3"

	c-c	e-e
P		
Q		
R		
S		

	Bill of Materials

Unit 28   ASSEMBLIES WITH CAST IRON WYES AND TEE-WYES

RELATED INFORMATION

Cast iron pipe assemblies use bends, wyes, and tee-wyes as well as some other fittings. The wyes and tee-wyes have three measurements to the center point. These lengths do not have the consistent pattern of threaded fittings. However, most manufacturers of cast fittings use the dimensions shown in the Data Sheets #12 through #19.

The new problem is to make the fittings allowances correctly, as the calculations for c-c are the same as in previous units showing similar diagrams with threaded pipe.

ASSIGNMENT

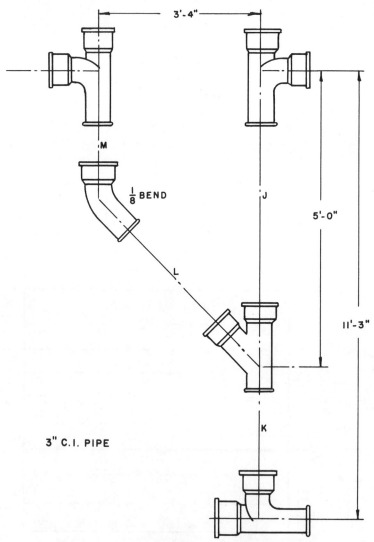

3' - 4"

⅛ BEND

M

L

J

K

5'-0"

11'-3"

3" C.I. PIPE

For each diagram:

  a. Solve for c-c and e-e lengths of each lettered pipe.

  b. Write an order list for fittings and pipe.

  c. Compute the pounds of lead required to assemble.

	c-c	e-e
J		
K		
L		
M		

Bill of Materials	

Lbs. Lead Required _____

74

	c-c	e-e
N		
O		
P		

	Bill of Materials	

Lbs. of Lead Required _____

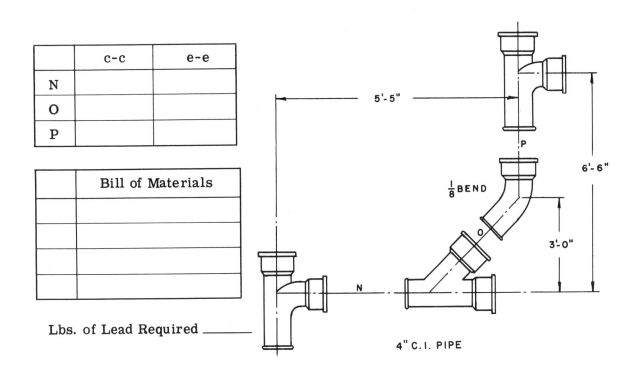

4" C.I. PIPE

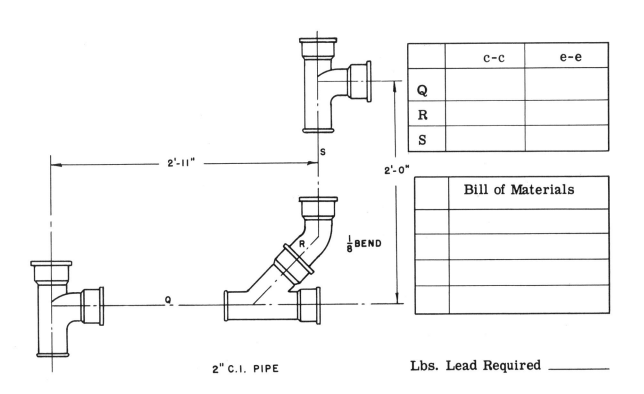

	c-c	e-e
Q		
R		
S		

	Bill of Materials	

2" C.I. PIPE

Lbs. Lead Required _____

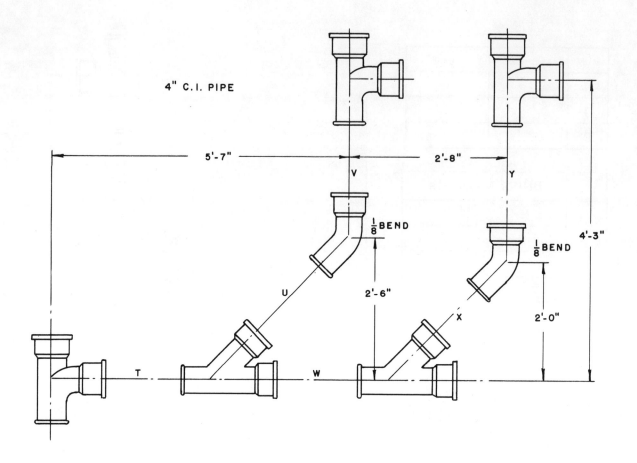

4" C.I. PIPE

5'-7"   2'-8"

V   Y

⅛ BEND   ⅛ BEND

U   4'-3"

2'-6"   X

T   W   2'-0"

	c-c	e-e
T		
U		
V		
W		
X		
Y		

	Bill of Materials

Lbs. Lead Required _____

Unit 29   SINGLE LOOP

RELATED INFORMATION

A loop is waste and vent piping to connect a fixture at some distance from the stack. The stack is the main riser of the waste piping and extends through the roof to provide for venting. It is called a soil stack if a water closet is connected into it.

The stack is often cast iron while the loop is steel pipe with threaded fittings. Thus there can be a connection of steel pipe into a hub. Such a connection permits closing of the loop without using a union. The union is not acceptable on waste and vent lines. Both 1 1/2" and 2" steel pipe can be caulked into a 2" cast iron hub.

The new calculation is for the fittings allowance when a pipe connects between a threaded fitting and a hub. Since a loop is installed above and below a floor, the floor line is introduced into the diagram.

SAMPLE PROBLEM

Solve for c-c and e-e of lettered pipes.

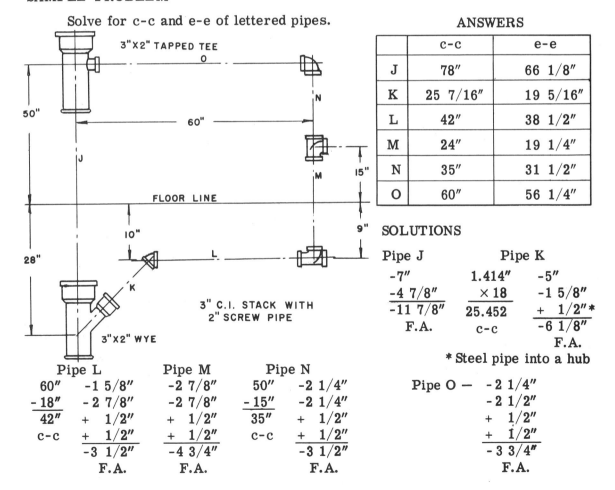

ANSWERS

	c-c	e-e
J	78"	66 1/8"
K	25 7/16"	19 5/16"
L	42"	38 1/2"
M	24"	19 1/4"
N	35"	31 1/2"
O	60"	56 1/4"

SOLUTIONS

Pipe J   Pipe K
-7"   1.414"   -5"
-4 7/8"   × 18   -1 5/8"
-11 7/8" 25.452   + 1/2"*
F.A.   c-c   -6 1/8"
                    F.A.
* Steel pipe into a hub

Pipe L   Pipe M   Pipe N
60"   -1 5/8"   -2 7/8"   50"   -2 1/4"
-18" -2 7/8"   -2 7/8"   -15" -2 1/4"
42"   + 1/2"   + 1/2"   35"   + 1/2"
c-c   + 1/2"   + 1/2"   c-c   + 1/2"
      -3 1/2"   -4 3/4"   -3 1/2"
      F.A.   F.A.   F.A.

Pipe O — - 2 1/4"
          - 2 1/2"
          + 1/2"
          + 1/2"
          - 3 3/4"
          F.A.

ASSIGNMENT

Solve for c-c and e-e for each lettered pipe in the following diagrams.

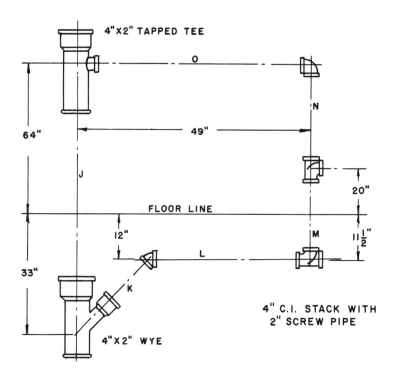

4"X2" TAPPED TEE

O

N

64"

49"

J

20"

FLOOR LINE

12"

11½"

33"

L

M

K

4" C.I. STACK WITH
2" SCREW PIPE

4"X2" WYE

	c-c	e-e
J		
K		
L		
M		
N		
O		

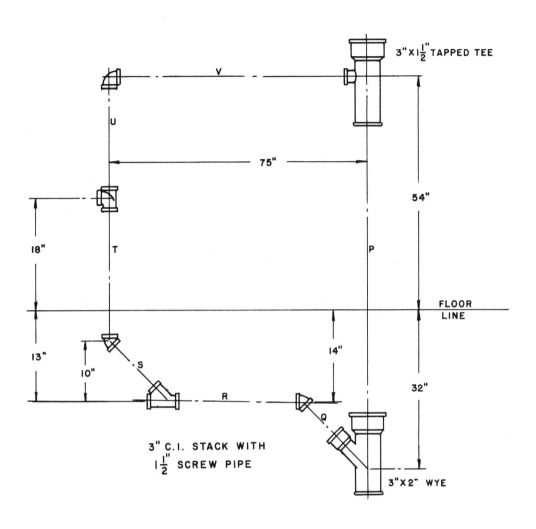

3"X1½" TAPPED TEE

V

U

75"

54"

18"

T

P

FLOOR
LINE

13"

S

10"

14"

32"

R

Q

3" C.I. STACK WITH
1½" SCREW PIPE

3"X2" WYE

	c-c	e-e
P		
Q		
R		
S		
T		
U		
V		

RELATED INFORMATION

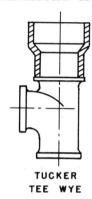

TUCKER
TEE WYE

The slip and caulk fittings often referred to as "Kennedy" or "Tucker" fittings are used to make the last connection in a loop or other waste piping where a union is not acceptable. The hub is used to make a caulked joint on steel or wrought iron pipe as this is a fitting for threaded pipe.

The pipe goes to the bottom of the second drop and lifts partly out of the second drop as it is screwed into the fitting at the other end of the pipe. The slip and caulk hub takes care of both thread-in allowances.

SAMPLE PROBLEM

Solve for c-c and e-e lengths of pipes J and K. The calculations for other pipes are previously covered.

ANSWERS

	c-c	e-e
J	23″	19 3/8″
K	33″	30″

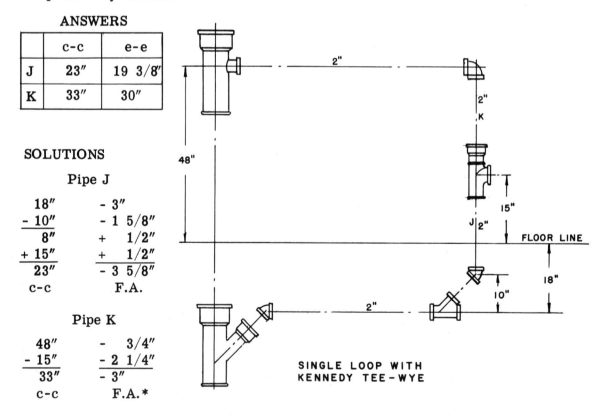

SINGLE LOOP WITH
KENNEDY TEE-WYE

SOLUTIONS

Pipe J

18″	- 3″
- 10″	- 1 5/8″
8″	+ 1/2″
+ 15″	+ 1/2″
23″	- 3 5/8″
c-c	F.A.

Pipe K

48″	- 3/4″
- 15″	- 2 1/4″
33″	- 3″
c-c	F.A.*

* Thread-in taken care of by slip and caulk hub.

80

ASSIGNMENT

Solve for c-c and e-e of each lettered pipe.

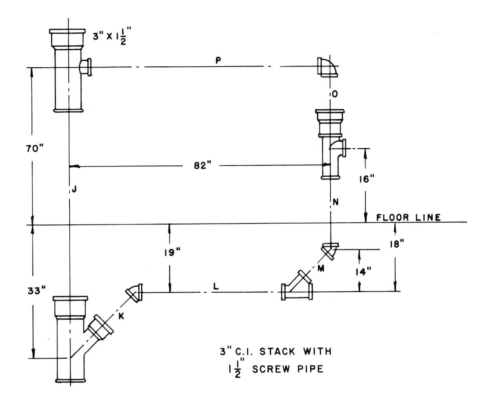

3" C.I. STACK WITH
$1\frac{1}{2}$" SCREW PIPE

	c-c	e-e
J		
K		
L		
M		
N		
O		
P		

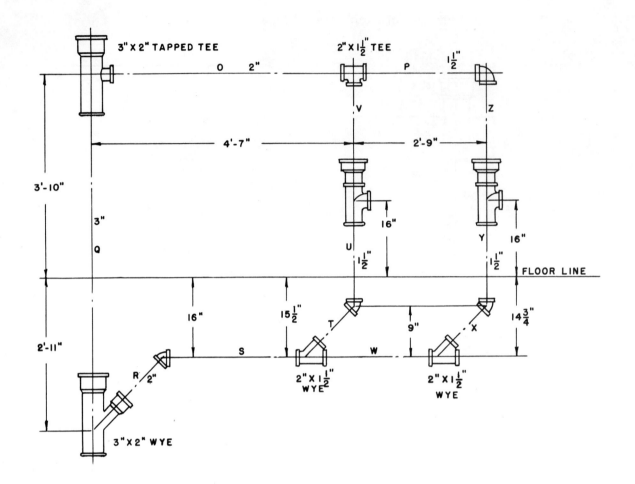

	c-c	e-e
Q		
R		
S		
T		
U		
V		

	c-c	e-e
W		
X		
Y		
Z		
P		
O		

Unit 31 GRADE, DROP AND RUN

RELATED INFORMATION

Grade indicates a slight amount out of level. Sometimes it is called pitch, but by either name the purpose is to allow the waste line to carry solids better than a true horizontal pipe could. A grade is much smaller than an offset.

Drainage fittings such as tee-wyes and 90° ells are tapped to give a grade of 1/4 inch per foot. This means that the horizontal drain line is out of level by 1/4 of an inch for each foot of run. Some plumbing codes specify a minimum grade of 1/8 inch per foot.

The drop is the total amount out of level. Thus at 1/4 inch per foot, the drop would be one inch if continued for four feet.

FORMULAS

<u>Drop</u> is amount out of level in inches.

$$\text{Drop} = \text{grade} \times \text{run}$$

<u>Grade</u> is rate of slope in inches per foot.

$$\text{Grade} = \frac{\text{drop}}{\text{run}}$$

<u>Run</u> is horizontal length in feet.

SAMPLE PROBLEM 1

How much drop for 18 feet of run at 1/8″ per foot grade?

SOLUTION

Drop = grade × run   Drop = 1/8″ × 18 = 2 1/4″   **Ans.**

SAMPLE PROBLEM 2

A drop of 5 inches in 22 feet is what grade to the nearest 32nd inch?

SOLUTION

$\text{Grade} = \dfrac{\text{drop}}{\text{run}}$ $\text{Grade} = \dfrac{5}{22}$ $\text{Grade} = .227 = \dfrac{7}{32}$ inches/ft.   **Ans.**

MATHEMATICS FOR PLUMBERS GRADE, DROP AND RUN

ASSIGNMENT

Complete the following for drop or for grade as indicated by blank space.

	Run	Grade	Drop
1.	12'	1/4"/ft.	
2.	27'	1/4"/ft.	
3.	5'	1/8"/ft.	
4.	35'	5/32"/ft.	
5.	26'		5"
6.	46'		6 1/2"
7.	72'		9 3/4"
8.	84"	1/8"/ft.	

Unit 32   LOOPS WITH GRADE

RELATED INFORMATION

Pipes at a grade are slightly longer than the horizontal run. The difference amounts to about .005 inches for 8 feet of run when the grade is 1/8 inch per foot. So for all plumbing purposes the run and the pipe with grade are the same length.

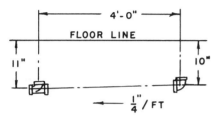

However, the vertical pipes that connect to the pipe with grade are changed in length by the drop. If two risers four feet apart connect to a pipe at 1/4 inch per foot grade, then the drop is 1 inch. Thus, one riser must be 1 inch longer, or shorter, than the other.

SAMPLE PROBLEM

Compute the c-c lengths for pipes J, K, L, and M. The e-e lengths methods are included in previous units. Pipe J should have a drop. The grade is usually not specified for vent runs but is given for practice solutions.

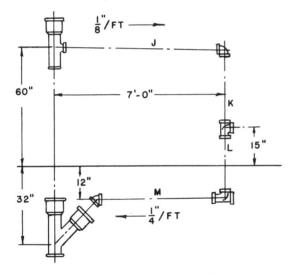

ANSWERS

	c-c
J	7'-0"
K	44 1/8"
L	25 3/4"
M	5'-4"

Pipe M

Offset = 32" - 12" = 20"   7'-0"
45°, therefore run =20"   - 1'-8"
                              5'-4"

SOLUTIONS

Pipe K

Drop of J = 7 × 1/8" = 7/8"

    60"
   - 15"
    45" with no drop
   - 7/8"
    44 7/8" with drop

Pipe L

Drop of M = 5 × 1/4" = 1 1/4"

    15"
   + 12"
    27" if no drop
   - 1 1/4"
    25 3/4" so that M has drop

85

ASSIGNMENT

Solve for c-c and e-e lengths of each lettered pipe.

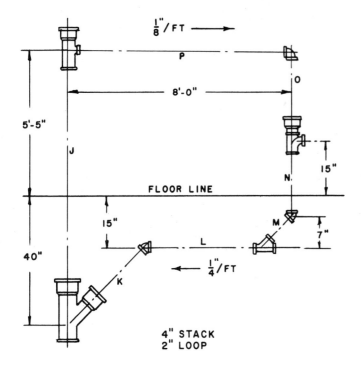

	c-c	e-e
J		
K		
L		
M		
N		
O		
P		

4" STACK
2" LOOP

	c-c	e-e
Q		
R		
S		
T		
U		
V		
W		

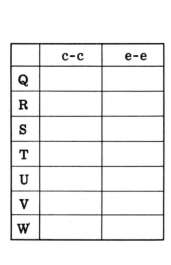

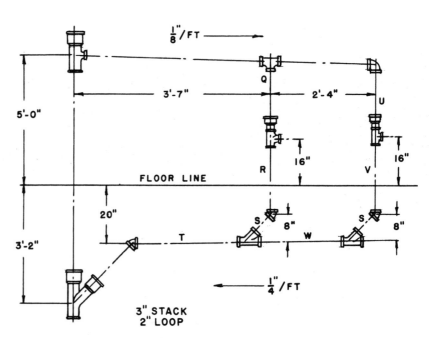

3" STACK
2" LOOP

Unit 33   ELEVATIONS AND GRADE

RELATED INFORMATION

An elevation is a certain distance above or below a fixed point. Land or geographic elevations are distances above, or below sea level. The architect may specify building elevations based on sea level but often a number, as 100.00 feet, is used as a reference or "bench mark". The bench mark is some nonmoving spot as on the curb and it is called 100.00 feet elevation because the number is easy to add to, or subtract from. A first floor at elevation 103.50 feet would be 3 1/2 feet higher than the bench mark. A basement floor at elevation 94.00 feet would be 6 feet lower than the bench mark.

The surveyor or civil engineer uses elevation measurements in feet and decimal parts of a foot. One-hundredth (.01) feet is the smallest elevation difference. The plumber uses feet, inches, and nearest eighth of an inch in elevation measure. An eighth of an inch is very nearly the same as a hundredth of a foot. It may be necessary for the plumber to convert engineering and building trade elevations as both are used.

A pipe at a grade changes elevation. The plumber needs to determine the elevations of points on house sewers and house drains.

SAMPLE PROBLEMS

1. Convert 8'-4 5/8" to engineer's measure.

8'	is		8. ft.
4 5/8"	is	$\frac{4.625}{12}$	.38 ft.
			8.38 ft. Ans.

Also,

8'	is	8. ft.
4"	is	.33 ft.
5/8"	is	.05 ft.
		8.38 ft. Ans.

2. Convert 94.28 ft. to builder's measure.

94 ft.	is	94 ft.
.28 × 12	is 3.36"=	3 3/8 in.
		94'-3 3/8" Ans.

Also,

94. ft.	is	94 ft.
.25 ft.	is	3 in.
.03 ft.	is	3/8 in.
		94'-3 3/8" Ans.

3. BM is 100.00 ft. elevation.

Basement floor is 94.70 ft. elevation.

First floor is 102.95 ft. elevation.

     a. How far below the BM is the basement floor?

     b. How far above the BM is the first floor?

     c. How far from basement floor to first floor?

      a. 100.00

        - 94.70

          5.30 ft. below BM or 5'-3 5/8" <u>Ans.</u>

         (.30' = .25' + .05'; .25' = 3"; .05' = 5/8")

      b. 102.95

       - 100.00

          2.95 ft. above BM or 2'-11 3/8" <u>Ans.</u>

        (.95' is 1' - .05'; thus, 5/8" less than 12")

      c. 102.95

       - 94.70

          8.25 ft. between or 8'-3" <u>Ans.</u>

4. A house drain has a run of 30 feet at a grade of 1/8 inch per foot. The low end has elevation of 93.50 ft. What elevation is the high end?

      $30 \times 1/8''$ = 3 3/4" difference in elevation

      93.50 = 93'-6"

          +   3 3/4"

          93'-9 3/4" <u>Ans.</u>

   Also, 1/8" is about .01 ft., so

     $.01 \times 30$ = .30 ft. difference in elevation

          93.50

       +   .30

         93.80 ft. <u>Ans.</u>

(Note: The two answers are not exactly equal because 1/8 inch is a little larger than .01 feet. For purposes of grade either answer is acceptable.)

ASSIGNMENT

A. Convert each measurement to engineer's measure.

    1. 18'-6" _____

    2. 15'-5 1/2" _____

    3. 32'-9" _____

    4. 33'-10" _____

    5. 35'-11 1/4" _____

B. Convert each measurement to builder's measure

    1. 84.27' _____

    2. 93.08' _____

    3. 106.71' _____

    4. 123.44' _____

    5. 156.92' _____

C. Some building elevations follow: BM 100.00, basement floor 94.20, first floor 103.75, second floor 113.00.

    1. How far below the BM is the basement floor? _____

    2. How far above the BM is the first floor? _____

    3. Height from basement floor to first floor? _____

    4. Height from first floor to second floor? _____

D. The low end of a house drain has an elevation of 91.55'. The grade is 1/8" per foot.

    1. What is elevation of a fitting 10' from the low point? _____

    2. What is the elevation of a fitting 25' from the low point? _____

Unit 34   ELEVATIONS IN A PLAN VIEW PIPE DIAGRAM

RELATED INFORMATION

Most of the pipe diagrams shown in this book have been drawn as elevation views. Some of them would only be installed in walls and are diagramed in the proper position. However, pipe is run under ground or under floors and is then best shown in a plan view. House sewers and house drains are drawn as plan view pipe diagrams.

Since the pipe has grade there is a change in elevation. The elevation does not show in a plan view so a note is made of the elevation of points along the pipe.

Most pipes are measured to a center line but sewers and house drains show elevations measured to the invert of the sewer. The invert is the inside and bottom of the pipe. The advantages of measuring to the invert of the pipe, which is a solid surface, are easily seen.

SAMPLE PROBLEM

Compute the c-c lengths for pipes J, K, L, and M and the elevations of points A, B, C, and D. These points are on the invert of the pipe directly under the inter-section of the centerlines.

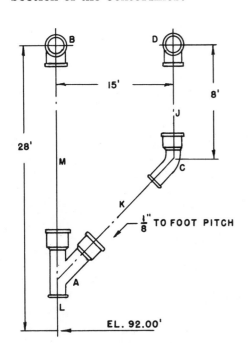

ANSWERS

	c-c
J	8'
K	21.21 or 21'-2 1/2"
L	5'
M	23'

Pipe K	Pipe M	Pipe L
1.414	8'	28'
× 15'	+15'	- 23'
21.210'	23'	5'

ANSWERS

Elevations			
A	92.05'	C	92.27'
B	92.29'	D	92.35'

Elevation A   L is 5' long
                     $5 \times 1/8'' = 5/8''$ elevation change, or .05'

Elevation B $28 \times 1/8'' = 28/8 = 3\ 1/2''$ or .29 feet

Elevation C $26 \times 1/8'' = 26/8 = 3\ 1/4''$ or .27 feet

Elevation D $34 \times 1/8'' = 34/8 = 4\ 1/4''$ or .35 feet

ASSIGNMENT

1. Compute the c-c lengths of pipes J, K, and L and the elevations for points A, B, and C in the plan of the house drain.

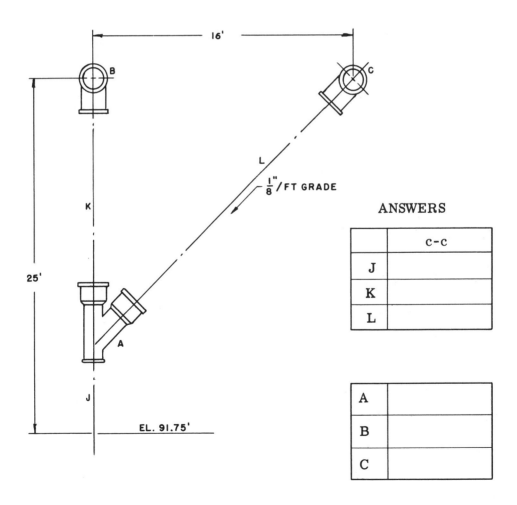

ANSWERS

	c-c
J	
K	
L	

A	
B	
C	

2. Compute the c-c lengths for pipes J, K, L, M, and N. Compute the elevations at points A, B, C, and D.

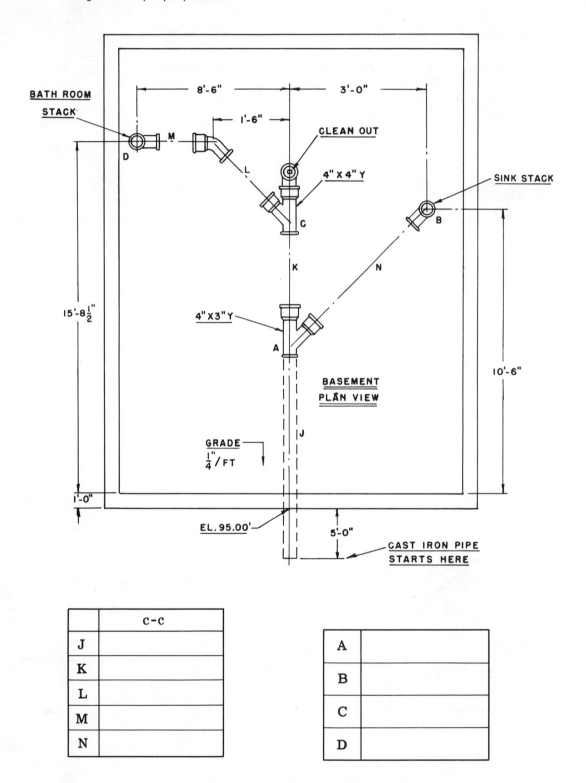

	c-c
J	
K	
L	
M	
N	

A	
B	
C	
D	

Unit 35   TUBING

RELATED INFORMATION

Copper tubing has good performance and long life for water (pressure) lines and for waste line plumbing. For copper plumbing the tubing is designed for pressure use or for drainage, waste and vent use. The lighter weight tube is less costly than that designed to hold greater pressures. The copper tube is connected to the fitting by a soldering operation. Tubing of plastic or composition materials has some plumbing uses and may gain greater acceptance in the future.

Copper tubing is made in four weights called types. The types are K, L, M, and D.W.V. as shown by the following diagrams and table of information.

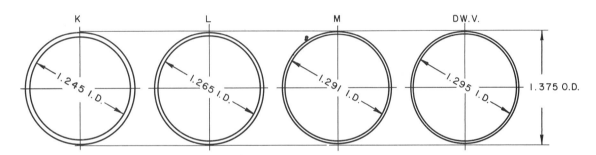

Type	K	L	M	D.W.V.
Recommended for	Underground and interior service	Interior service	Hot water heating. Drainage Waste or vent	Drainage, waste and vent service
Available in	Hard or soft temper	Hard or soft temper	Hard temper	Hard temper

The cross sections show the inside and outside diameters of 1 1/4″ nominal size copper tubing. The four types have the same outside diameter. Hard temper tubing is available in 20′ straight lengths while soft temper tubing is in coils as long as 100′ for the smaller sizes.

Nominal Size

Tubing is available in nominal sizes similar to the nominal sizes of threaded pipe. The nominal size of tubing is an approximation of the inside diameter. The outside diameter is 0.125″ greater than the nominal size.

SAMPLE PROBLEM

Compute the wall thickness for K-type tube of 1 1/4″ diameter. Refer to Data #24, Appendix page 190.

SOLUTION

Step 1: Determine O.D.   1.375″

Step 2: Determine I.D.   1.245″

Step 3: Subtract I.D. from O.D.   0.130″

Step 4: Divide by 2   0.065″ <u>Ans.</u>

ASSIGNMENT

Answer the following questions.

1. Compute the wall thickness for 3″ D.W.V. type copper tube. _____

2. Compute the wall thickness for 3″ L-type copper tube. _____

3. Which two types of copper tubing would be recommended for water supply inside a house? _____

4. What is the advantage of soft temper K-type tube over hard temper K-type tube for a water supply installed in a ditch? _____

_____

_____

5. Would K-type tube give satisfactory service on D.W.V. use? _____

   Give a reason for your answer. _____

_____

6. Would M-type tube be expected to be satisfactory for interior water lines?

_____

   Give a reason for your answer. _____

_____

_____

_____

Unit 36   ALLOWANCE FOR FITTINGS

RELATED INFORMATION

Fittings for copper tubing have a solder cup to make the connection to the tube. For pressure plumbing, such as water lines, the solder cup is deeper than for D.W.V. fittings. The D.W.V. fittings are also of lighter weight than pressure fittings. This is an economy in cost and in use of copper. The method of making allowance for fittings is the same for all copper-to-copper fittings.

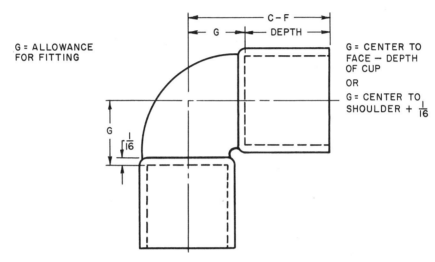

The allowance for a copper fitting may be made by one of two methods. In the first, the fitting is considered as similar to the threaded fitting. Thus, the allowance for fitting equals a center-to-face measurement minus a depth of solder cup. Both of these measurements can be made from the fitting.

The usual practice is to measure somewhat like the hub end of a cast iron fitting. The measurement is made from the centerline to 1/16" beyond the shoulder. The tables in the Appendix show the allowance for fittings as dimension "G" in the diagram. They are taken from manufacturers' catalogs and are to be used for the problems in this text. Measure the fitting on the job!

SAMPLE PROBLEM

Solve for e-e length of pipe K.

Step 1   Allowance for 90°ell from data #25, 1/2", Appendix page 191.

Step 2   Allowance for 45°ell, 1/4"

Step 3   Add the allowances, 3/4"

Step 4   10" - 3/4" = 9 1/4" = e-e   <u>Ans.</u>

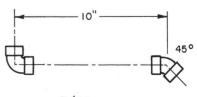

3/4" copper

ASSIGNMENT

Solve problems 1-5 for e-e length of tube required. Use the Allowance for Fittings Data #25, Appendix page 191.

	c-c	Tube	Ells	e-e
1.	18″	3/4″	90°	
2.	7′3″	3″	90°	
3.	31 1/2″	1 1/4″	90°-45°	
4.	43″	2″	90°-22 1/2°	
5.	6′9″	1 1/2″	90°-60°	

NOTE: Copper tube and fittings may be used for many of the problems in the following units of this text. This will not affect c-c answers.

Spaces are provided for e-e answers for both threaded and copper, or cast iron and copper where copper can be used as an alternate method.

The use of two materials in a problem allows a comparison of e-e answers. Also, problems may be solved for one e-e answer at the discretion of the instructor.

Unit 37   JUMPER OFFSETS

RELATED INFORMATION

A jumper offset is one that goes around a stack, tank, or other cylindrical object. The diagonals are always at 45° angles but the on-the-job measurements change the solution from the usual.

There are two different patterns of jumper offsets. One is made with two 45° ells and one 90° ell. The other uses four 45° ells.

There are four different solutions used in connection with various 45° diagonals. They are as follows:

1. Diagonal = 1.414 × offset

2. Offset = .707 × diagonal

3. Diagonal = 2 × side of secondary square

4. Use of .414 constant for 22 1/2° angle in some
    45° fitting diagrams.

In the calculation of the two patterns of jumper offsets, all four solutions are used.

SAMPLE PROBLEM 1

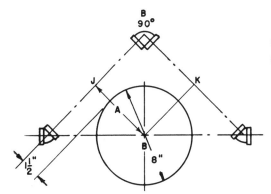

Solve for the c-c lengths of J and K. For the offset use two 45° ells and one 90° ell. On this problem the centerline of the cylindrical obstacle coincides with the centerline of the pipe.

ANSWERS

	c-c
J	11″
K	11″

SOLUTION

The distance A = radius + clearance.   A = 4″ + 1 1/2″ = 5 1/2″

But, A is the side of a secondary square so

J = 2 × A = 2 × 5 1/2″ = 11″ c-c <u>Ans.</u>

K also = 11″ c-c <u>Ans.</u>

The offset (B-B) = .707 × 11″ = 7 3/4″ <u>Ans.</u>

SAMPLE PROBLEM 2

Solve for c-c lengths of pipes J, K, L, and M. In this problem, the centerline of the obstacle does not coincide with the centerline of the pipe.

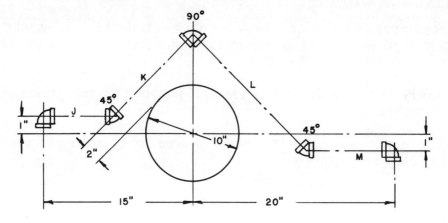

ANSWERS

	c-c
J	6 1/8″
K	12 9/16″
L	15 7/16″
M	9 1/16″

SOLUTION

Radius + clearance = 5″ + 2″ = 7″
1.414 × 1″ = 1.414″ = 1 7/16″

K = (2 × 7″) - 1 7/16″
K = 14″ - 1 7/16″ = 12 9/16″ <u>Ans.</u>

L = (2 × 7″) + 1 7/16″ = 15 7/16″ <u>Ans.</u>

Offset for K = .707 × 12 9/16″ = 8.88 = 8 7/8″
J = 15″ - 8 7/8″ = 6 1/8″   <u>Ans.</u>

Offset for L = .707 × 15 7/16″ = 10 15/16″
M = 20″ - 10 15/16″ = 9 1/16″   <u>Ans.</u>

SAMPLE PROBLEM 3

Solve for c-c of pipes J, K, L, M, and N.

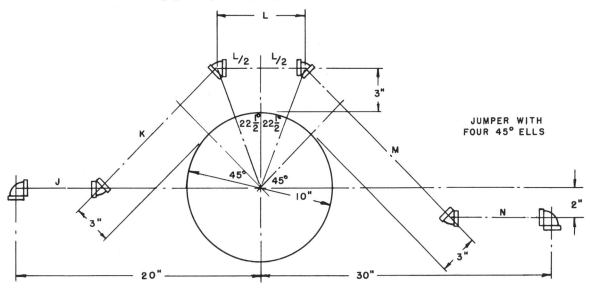

ANSWERS

	c-c
J	8 11/16″
K	11 5/16″
L	6 5/8″
M	14 1/8″
N	16 11/16″

SOLUTION

The offset for K = radius + clearance
Offset for K = 5 + 3 = 8″
K = 1.414 × 8″ = 11.312 = 11 5/16″   Ans.

L/2 = .414 × 8″ = 3.312 = 3 5/16″
L = 2 × 3 5/16″ = 6 5/8″   Ans.

The offset for M = radius + clearance + 2″ = 10″
M = 1.414 × 10″ = 14.14″ = 14 1/8″   Ans.

J = 20″- (8″+ 3 5/16″) = 20″ - 11 5/16″ = 8 11/16″   Ans.

N = 30″ - (10″ + 3 5/16″) = 30″ - 13 5/16″ = 16 11/16″   Ans.

ASSIGNMENT

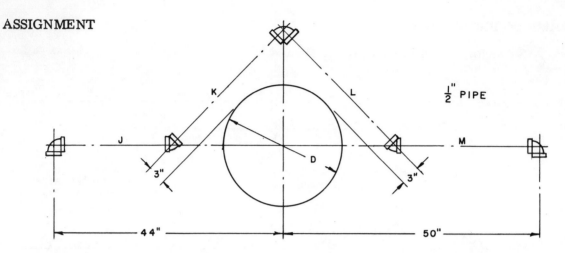

1. Solve for c-c and e-e of pipes J, K, L, and M with D = 12".

	c-c	e-e	e-e copper
J			
K			
L			
M			

2. Solve for c-c and e-e of pipes J, K, L, and M with D = 20".

	c-c	e-e	e-e copper
J			
K			
L			
M			

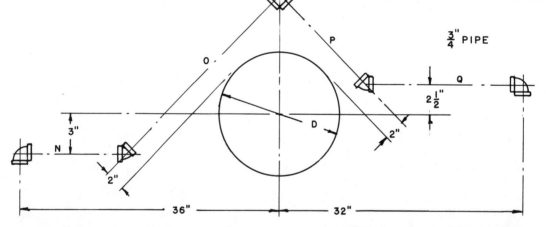

3. Solve for c-c and e-e of pipes N, O, P, and Q with D = 9".

	c-c	e-e	e-e copper
N			
O			
P			
Q			

4. Solve for c-c and e-e of pipes N, O, P, and Q with D = 24".

	c-c	e-e	e-e copper
N			
O			
P			
Q			

5. Solve for c-c and e-e of pipes R, S, T, U, and V with D = 5″.

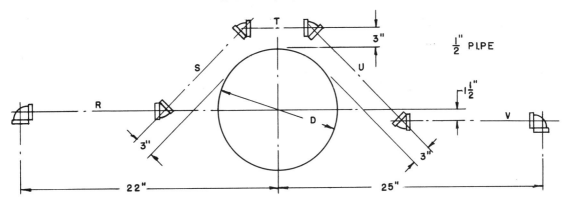

	c-c	e-e	e-e copper
R			
S			
T			
U			
V			

6. Solve for c-c and e-e lengths of pipes R, S, T, U, and V using the diagram of Problem 5 with D = 15″.

	c-c	e-e	e-e copper
R			
S			
T			
U			
V			

Unit 38   45° OFFSETS IN PARALLEL

RELATED INFORMATION

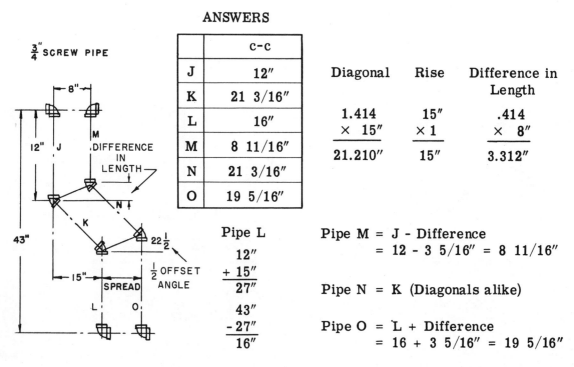

Parallel offsets are used because of neat appearance that saves space and allows room for installation of pipe covering. Two or more pipe assemblies can be installed in parallel or equal spread design.

The parallel offsets always have parallel angles one-half of the offset angle.

In all but a special case the diagonals are alike.

One assembly is computed as a simple offset. The second, and succeeding assemblies, have certain differences in length compared to the first. The difference in length is computed from the "spread" or distance between pipe assemblies.

SAMPLE PROBLEM

Solve for c-c of pipes J, K, L and M, N, and O. Calculations for e-e are omitted for clarity of new ideas.

ANSWERS

	c-c
J	12"
K	21 3/16"
L	16"
M	8 11/16"
N	21 3/16"
O	19 5/16"

Diagonal	Rise	Difference in Length
1.414	15"	.414
× 15"	× 1	× 8"
21.210"	15"	3.312"

Pipe L
12"
+ 15"
27"

43"
- 27"
16"

Pipe M = J - Difference
       = 12 - 3 5/16" = 8 11/16"

Pipe N = K (Diagonals alike)

Pipe O = L + Difference
       = 16 + 3 5/16" = 19 5/16"

ASSIGNMENT

   1. Solve for c-c and e-e lengths of each pipe shown in diagram below.

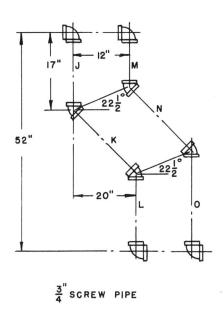

$\frac{3}{4}"$ SCREW PIPE

	c-c	e-e	e-e copper
J			
K			
L			
M			
N			
O			

   2. Solve for c-c and e-e lengths of each pipe shown in diagram below.

	c-c	e-e	e-e copper
J			
K			
L			
M			
N			
O			

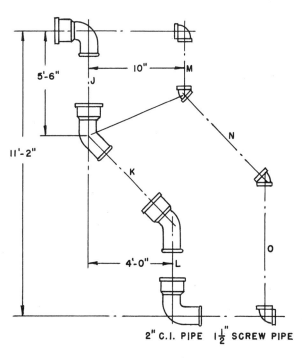

2" C.I. PIPE $1\frac{1}{2}"$ SCREW PIPE

103

3. Solve for c-c and e-e lengths of the pipes shown in the following diagram.

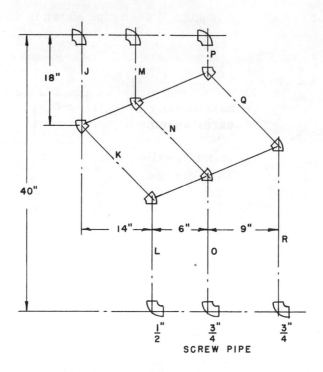

	c-c	e-e	e-e copper
J			
K			
L			
M			
N			
O			
P			
Q			
R			

Unit 39   SPECIAL CASE OF 45° OFFSETS IN PARALLEL

RELATED INFORMATION

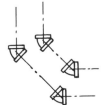

The special case of 45° parallel offsets uses two 45° or 1/8 bend fittings to turn a 90° turn. The pipe assemblies are somewhat like portions of a circle having the same center but different radii. The assembly farther from the center has longer pipes than the nearer assembly.

The same parallel angles, 22 1/2°, as for the usual 45° parallel offsets are used. Thus the .414 constant times the spread gives the difference in length. The diagonals, however, are not alike but differ by two times the difference in length.

SAMPLE PROBLEM

Solve for c-c of pipes J, K, L and M, N, and O.

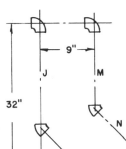

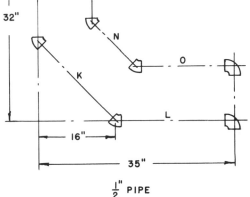

$\frac{1}{2}''$ PIPE

Diagonal: $16'' \times 1.414 = 22.624''$

Rise: $16'' \times 1 = 16''$

Difference in Length: $9'' \times .414 = 3.726''$

ANSWERS

	c-c		c-c
J	16″	M	12 1/4″
K	22 5/8″	N	15 1/8″
L	19″	O	15 1/4″

Pipe J = 32″ - 16″ = 16″

Pipe L = 35″ - 16″ = 19″

Pipe M = J - Difference
= 16″ - 3 3/4″
= 12 1/4″

Pipe N = K - (2 × Difference)
= 22 5/8″ - (2 × 3 3/4″)
= 15 1/8″

Pipe O = L - Difference
= 19 - 3 3/4″
= 15 1/4″

105

ASSIGNMENT

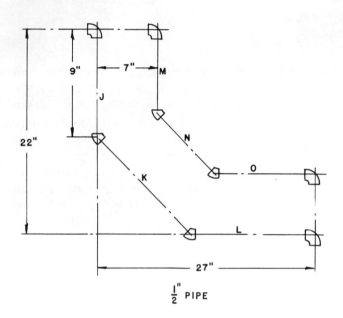

$\frac{1}{2}$" PIPE

1. Solve for c-c and e-e for each pipe length shown left.

	c-c	e-e	e-e copper
J			
K			
L			
M			
N			
O			

2. Solve for c-c and e-e lengths for each pipe length shown below.

	c-c	e-e	e-e copper
J			
K			
L			
M			
N			
O			
P			
Q			
R			

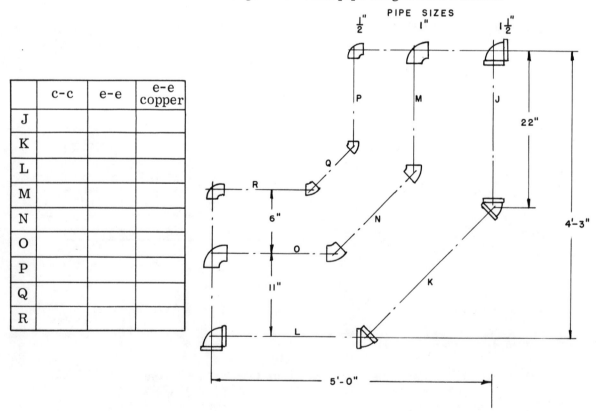

RELATED INFORMATION

The difference in length method can be applied to 90° fittings as well as to the other angles. The parallel angle for 90° fittings is 45° and the difference in length equals the spread.

A more challenging problem is to use both 90° and 45° turns in a parallel assembly. Thus there is at least one pipe affected by both differences in length.

SAMPLE PROBLEM

Solve for c-c lengths of pipes J, K, L, M and N, O, P, Q.

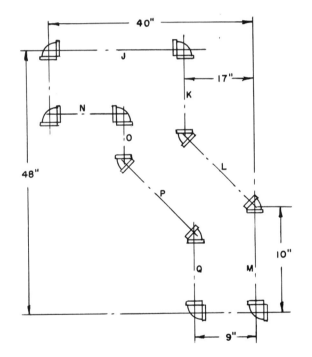

ANSWERS

	c-c		c-c
J	23″	N	14″
K	21″	O	15 3/4″
L	24″	P	24″
M	10″	Q	6 1/4″

Diagonal: $17″ \times 1.414 = 24.038″$

Rise: $17″ \times 1 = 17″$

Differences in Length:
$1 \times 9″ = 9″$
$9″ \times .414 = 3.726″$

Pipe J = 40″ - 17″ = 23″   Pipe K = 10″ + 17″ = 27″   Pipe L = Diagonal
                                                    48″ - 27″ = 21″   = 24″

Pipe N = J - 9″ = 14″   Pipe O = K - 9″ + 3 3/4″ = 15 3/4″

Pipe P = L = 24″   Pipe Q = M - 3 3/4″ = 6 1/4″

ASSIGNMENT

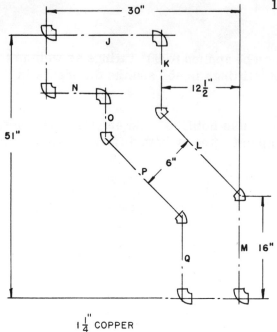

$1\frac{1}{4}$" COPPER

1. Solve for c-c and e-e lengths of each pipe shown left.

	c-c	e-e copper
J		
K		
L		
M		
N		
O		
P		
Q		

2. Solve for c-c and e-e lengths of each pipe shown right.

	c-c	e-e copper
J		
K		
L		
M		
N		
O		
P		
Q		

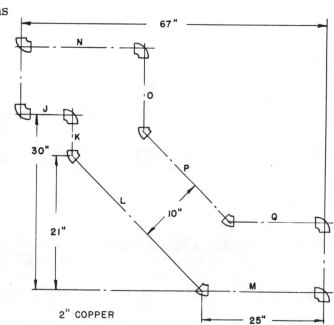

2" COPPER

Unit 41   VARIOUS OFFSETS IN PARALLEL

RELATED INFORMATION

All the various offset angles can be used in parallel assemblies. The rules that the parallel angle is half of the fitting angle, and the diagonals are alike, always apply. Of course a different angle requires a different set of constants.

The table in Data #22, Appendix, gives information for all fitting angles as used in parallel. A study of this table will show that only the difference in length constants are new to our calculations. The constants for diagonal and rise have been used with the simple offsets.

SAMPLE PROBLEM

Solve for c-c length of each pipe.   60° offsets in parallel.

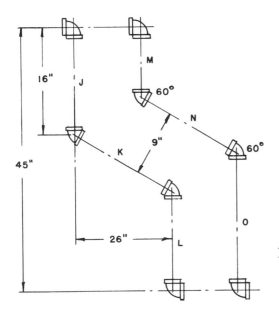

ANSWERS

	c-c
J	16″
K	30″
L	14″
M	10 13/16″
N	30″
O	19 3/16″

Diagonal	Rise	Difference in
1.154	.577	Length
× 26″	× 26″	.577
30.004″	15.002″	× 9″
		5.193″

Pipe L = 16″ + 15″ = 31″
45″ - 31″ = 14″

Pipe M = L - Difference
M = 16 - 5 3/16″
M = 10 13/16″

Pipe O = L + Difference
O = 14″ + 5 3/16″
O = 19 3/16″

ASSIGNMENT

1. Solve for c-c and e-e lengths of each pipe shown in the 60° parallel offset diagram.

	c-c	e-e copper
J		
K		
L		
M		
N		
O		

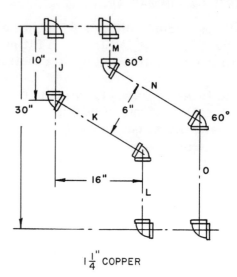

$1\frac{1}{4}"$ COPPER

2. Solve for c-c and e-e lengths of each pipe shown in the 22 1/2° parallel offset diagram.

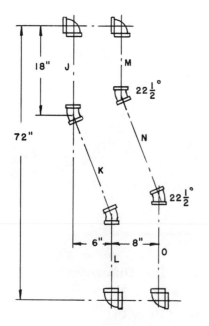

$1\frac{1}{2}"$ COPPER

	c-c	e-e copper
J		
K		
L		
M		
N		
O		

110

3. Solve for c-c and e-e lengths of each pipe shown in the 11 1/4° parallel offset diagram.

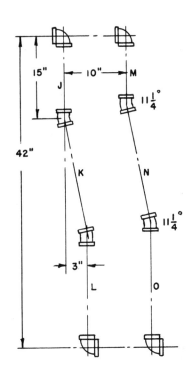

	c-c	e-e copper
J		
K		
L		
M		
N		
O		

2" COPPER

4. Solve for c-c lengths of each pipe shown in the 1/5 bend parallel offset diagram. Note: There is no 72° fitting in copper. Therefore copper is not an alternate for this diagram.

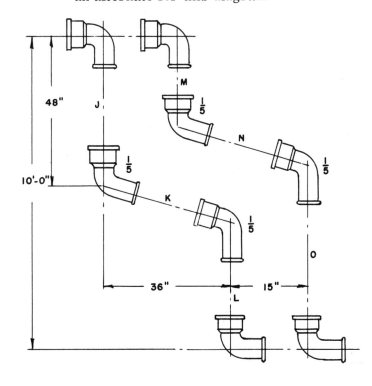

	c-c
J	
K	
L	
M	
N	
O	

Unit 42   ROLLING OFFSETS

RELATED INFORMATION

The rolling offset is a three-dimensional diagram. It represents a diagonal in a box. Rolling offsets can be made with two 45° fittings, with two 60° fittings, or with any two fittings of the same angle.

The entire solution of the rolling offset depends upon combining the rise and offset into a single dimension called the true offset. The true offset and the setback become the two sides of the square, or rectangle, around the diagonal.

The square root solution for the true offset gives a little better accuracy than the usual layout solution. However, the layout solution should be practiced and is preferred because it gives a usable answer without square root. The average plumber does not use square root often enough to keep in practice.

None of the constants are different from those used in simple and parallel offsets.

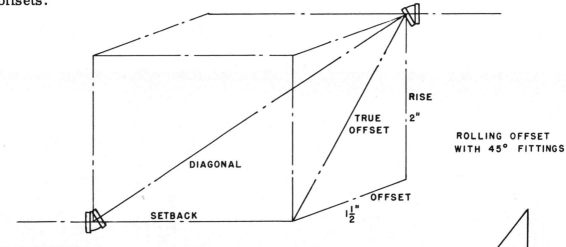

PROCEDURE

1. On the job measure offset and rise.

2. Determine true offset by formula or by layout method.

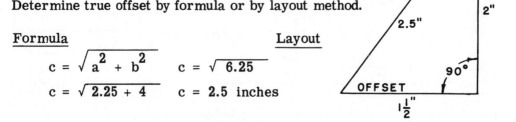

Formula	Layout
$c = \sqrt{a^2 + b^2}$	$c = \sqrt{6.25}$
$c = \sqrt{2.25 + 4}$	$c = 2.5$ inches

3. Multiply the true offset by the constants under the fitting angle in Data #23, Appendix, to compute the diagonal and setback.

SAMPLE PROBLEM

Solve for c-c lengths for pipes J, K, and L.

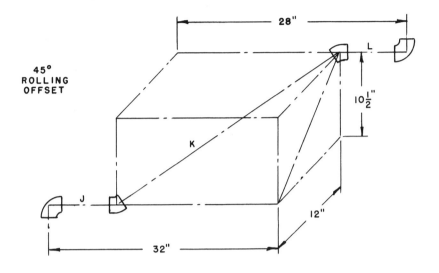

$$\text{True Offset} = \sqrt{\text{offset}^2 + \text{rise}^2}$$

$$= \sqrt{12^2 + 10.5^2}$$

$$= \sqrt{144 + 110.25}$$

$$= \sqrt{254.25}$$

$$\text{True Offset} = 15.94 \text{ or } 15\ 15/16''$$

ANSWERS

	c-c
J	16 1/16″
K	22 9/16″
L	12 1/16″

Setback = 1 × 15.94″ = 15.94″

J = 32″ - 15 15/16″ = 16 1/16″

L = 28″ - 15 15/16″ = 12 1/16″

K = 1.414 × 15.94 = 22 9/16″

ASSIGNMENT

1. Solve for c-c and e-e lengths of each pipe shown in the following diagram of a 45° rolling offset using 3/4″ pipe.

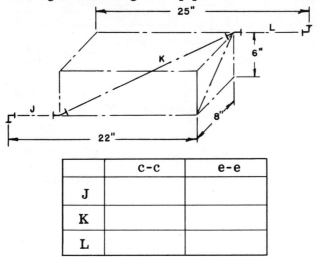

	c-c	e-e
J		
K		
L		

2. Solve for c-c and e-e lengths of each pipe using same diagram and pipe size as Problem 1, but with 11″ offset and 9″ rise.

	c-c	e-e
J		
K		
L		

3. Solve for c-c and e-e lengths of each pipe shown in the following diagram of a 60° rolling offset using 1 1/4″ pipe.

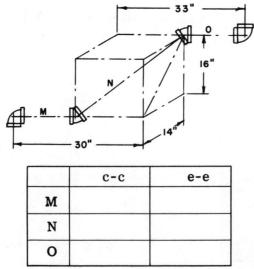

	c-c	e-e
M		
N		
O		

4. Solve for c-c and e-e lengths of each pipe shown in the following diagram of a 22 1/2° rolling offset using 2 1/2″ pipe.

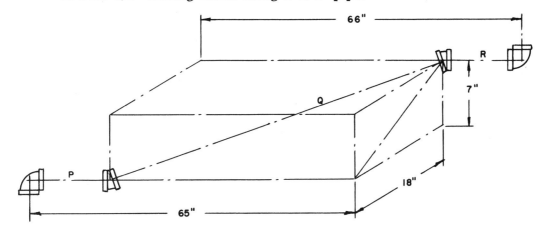

	c-c	e-e
P		
Q		
R		

Unit 43   COMBINATION OFFSETS

RELATED INFORMATION

The combination offset is like a rolling offset in that both are three-dimensional, therefore each represents a diagonal in a box.

The combination offset and the rolling offset differ in two ways. The combination connects pipes that are at right angles to each other and the rolling offset connects parallel pipes. Also, the combination offset gets its name from the use of fittings of different angles, usually a 45° and a 60° fitting, while the rolling offset uses any two fittings of the same angle.

There is only one angle at which combination offsets are practical in most plumbing. So it is unnecessary to solve for a true offset as each length in the box of the diagonal can be found by multiplying the offset by the proper constant.

The alternate directions shown in Figures 1 and 2 mean that a 60° fitting can be rotated to the new direction without any change in the diagonal or the box around the diagonal.

The three figures which follow do not represent all the possible combination offsets. Others have been devised for special purposes where the pipes connected by the diagonal are not at right angles to each other.

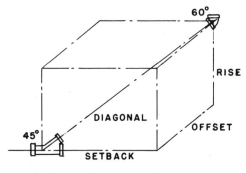

FIG.1   45° AND 60° COMBINATION OFFSET

Figure 1 shows a 45° and 60° combination, the most used of the combination offsets.

Measure the offset.

Rise = offset

Setback = 1.414 × offset

Diagonal = 2 × offset

Figure 2 is a different position or "alternate direction" of Figure 1.

Measure the offset.

Rise = 1.414 × offset

Setback = offset

Diagonal = 2 × offset

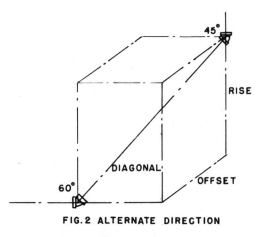

FIG.2 ALTERNATE DIRECTION

Figure 3 is a double combination connecting lines on two faces of a column or on two walls at a corner.

Measure O_1 and O_2

$R_1 = O_1$

$R_2 = O_2$

$d_1 = 1.414 \times O_1$

$d_2 = 1.414 \times O_2$

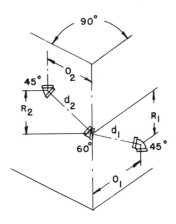

FIG. 3 DOUBLE COMBINATION

SAMPLE PROBLEMS

1. Solve for c-c lengths of each pipe in the diagram.

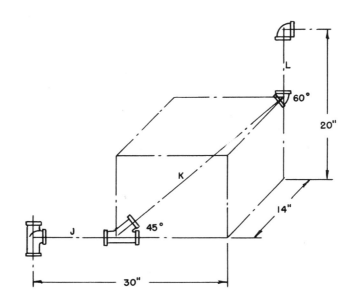

ANSWERS

	c-c
J	10 3/16″
K	28″
L	6″

Rise = offset = 14″

L = 20″ - 14″ = 6″   Ans.

K = 2 × 14″ = 28″   Ans.

Setback = 1.414 × 14″ = 19 13/16″

J = 30 - 19 13/16″ = 10 3/16″   Ans.

117

2. Solve for c-c lengths of each pipe in the following diagram.

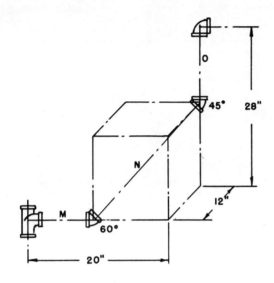

ANSWERS

	c-c
M	8″
N	24″
O	11″

Rise = 1.414 × 12″ = 17″

O = 28″ - 17″ = 11″   Ans.

N = 2 × 12″ = 24″   Ans.

Setback = offset = 12″

M = 20″ - 12″ = 8″   Ans.

3. Solve for c-c length of each pipe in the diagram below.

ANSWERS

	c-c
P	20″
Q	25 7/16″
R	21 3/16″
S	43″

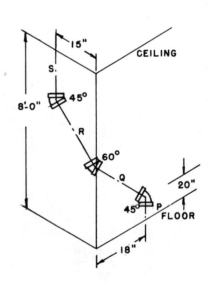

P = 20″ floor-to-center   Ans.

Q = 1.414 × 18″ = 25 7/16″   Ans.

R = 1.414 × 15″ = 21 3/16″   Ans.

S = (8′-0″) 96″ , - (15 + 18 + 20)

S = 96″ - 53″ = 43″ center-to-ceiling   Ans.

ASSIGNMENT

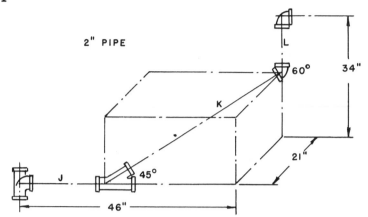

1. Solve for c-c and e-e lengths of each pipe shown above.

	c-c	e-e	e-e copper
J			
K			
L			

2. Solve for c-c and e-e lengths in diagram above, using 14 1/2″ offset.

	c-c	e-e	e-e copper
J			
K			
L			

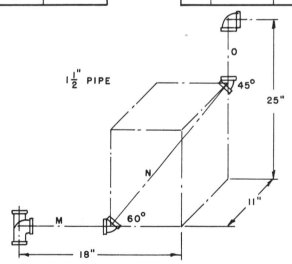

3. Solve for c-c and e-e lengths of each pipe shown above.

	c-c	e-e	e-e copper
M			
N			
O			

4. Solve for c-c and e-e lengths in diagram above using 9 1/2″ offset.

	c-c	e-e	e-e copper
M			
N			
O			

5. Solve for c-c and e-e lengths of each pipe shown in the following diagram.

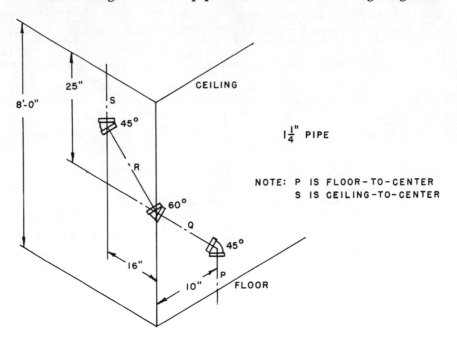

	c-c	e-e
P		
Q		
R		
S		

Unit 44   PIPE LENGTH BY LAYOUT

RELATED INFORMATION

The layout method for c-c lengths of pipe employs scale drawing. The layout is used to check a pipe length calculation, or to solve a problem for which math constants are not readily available.

The layout is simply a drawing with correctly measured angles and scale line lengths. The diagrams of this book have used measured angles to obtain the proper shapes, so a layout adds scale length to what has already been practiced. To be effective, the layout should be made to relatively large scale, 1/2″ = 1′-0″ or larger. To point this up, note the following illustration drawn to 1/4″ = 1′-0″. Pipe J measures 5/8″ and equals 30″ c-c. Pipe K is 7/16″ and equals 21″ c-c. (At 1/4″ scale, 1/16″ = 3″). Pipe O, however, is difficult to measure.

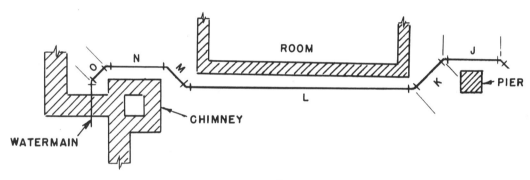

SCALE $\frac{1}{4}$″ = 1′- 0″

When the drawing is made to 1/2″ = 1′-0″ as in the portion on the right, Pipe O is seen to be 7/16″ and equals 10 1/2″ c-c. (At 1/2″ scale, 1/16″ = 1 1/2″).

Good drafting techniques give more accurate results than careless drawing. Cross-section paper is sometimes used as an aid in measuring, and in locating 45° lines.

In the problems of this unit, a 45° wye is used in a diagonal. The branch from a diagonal saves pipe in some situations.

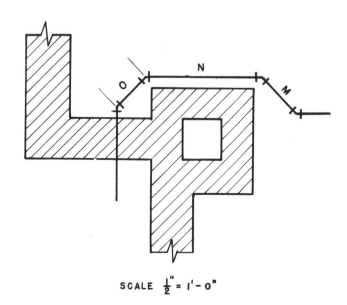

SCALE $\frac{1}{2}$″ = 1′- 0″

121

ASSIGNMENT

The plan view pipe diagrams used in Problems 1, 2, and 3 which follow have a stack at A, and risers at B and C. Dimensions are for the inside of the room. Walls are 6″ thick.

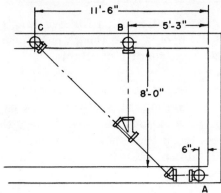

1. Make a layout using a scale of 1/2″ = 1′-0″ of the piping shown. Measure each c-c length. Compute each c-c length and compare with the measured lengths.

FIG. 1

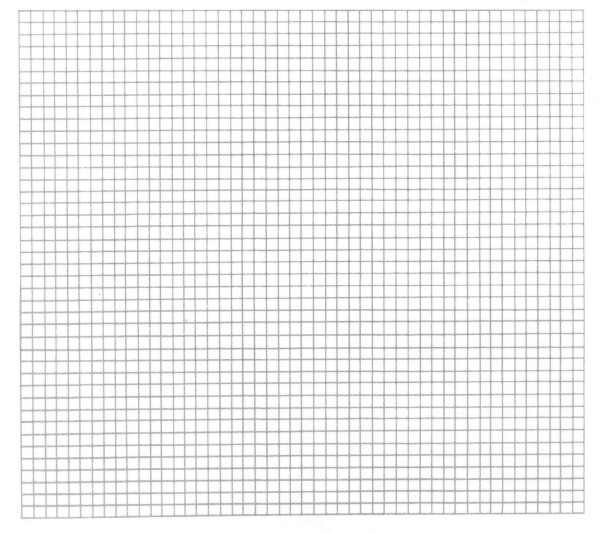

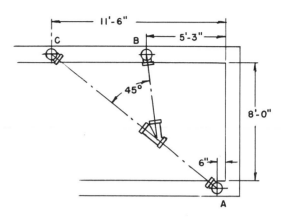

2. Make a layout of piping according to Figure 2.   Measure each c-c length. Compare the pipe and fittings needed with that for Prob. 1.

FIG. 2

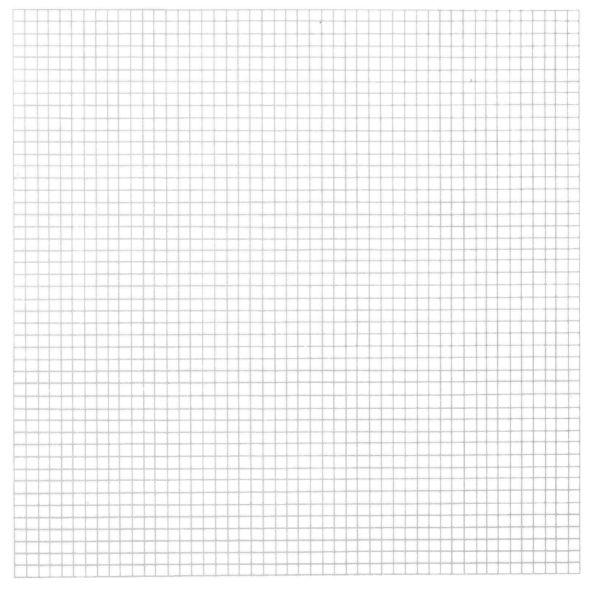

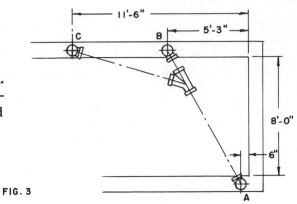

3. Make a layout of the piping shown. Measure the c-c lengths and compare to the pipe which is needed for Problem 2.

FIG. 3

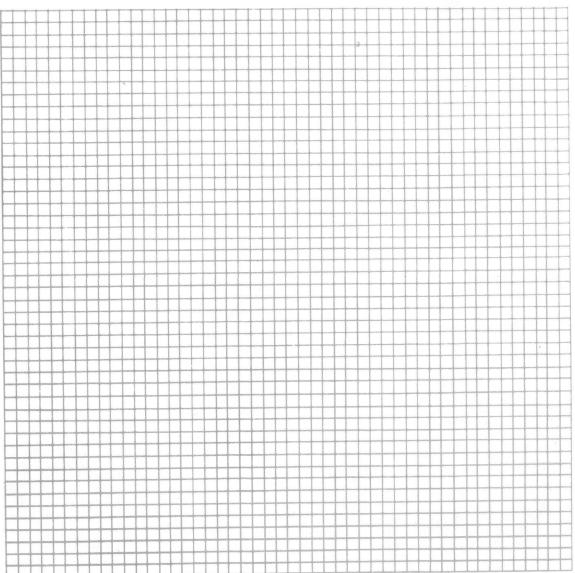

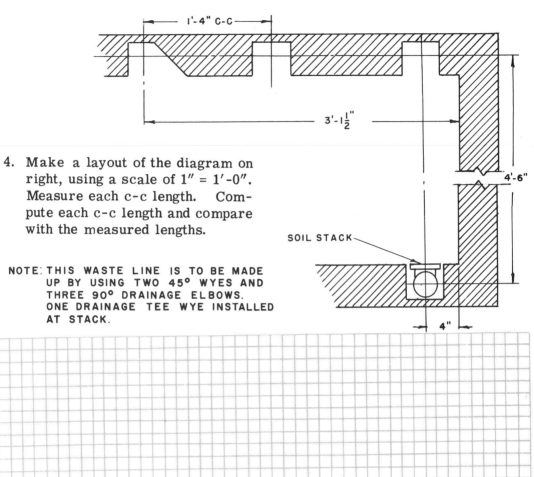

4. Make a layout of the diagram on right, using a scale of 1″ = 1′-0″. Measure each c-c length. Compute each c-c length and compare with the measured lengths.

NOTE: THIS WASTE LINE IS TO BE MADE UP BY USING TWO 45° WYES AND THREE 90° DRAINAGE ELBOWS. ONE DRAINAGE TEE WYE INSTALLED AT STACK.

5. Compute the measurements center-to-center by layout using scale $1/2'' = 1'-0''$ and using fittings listed. Compute also by calculation. Pipe is to run to the locations shown on sketch in the best direct manner, and is to have a cleanout at the end of main run.

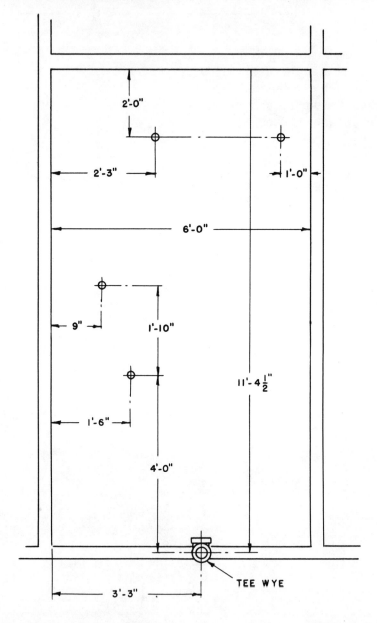

TEE WYE

USE - 2 - DRAINAGE WYES
" - 1 - " DBL. WYES } TO BE USED IN THE MAIN RUN AND BRANCHES.
" - 1 - " 45° ELBOW }
    - 4 - " 90° ELBOWS { TO BE USED AT THE END OF EACH BRANCH FACING UP.

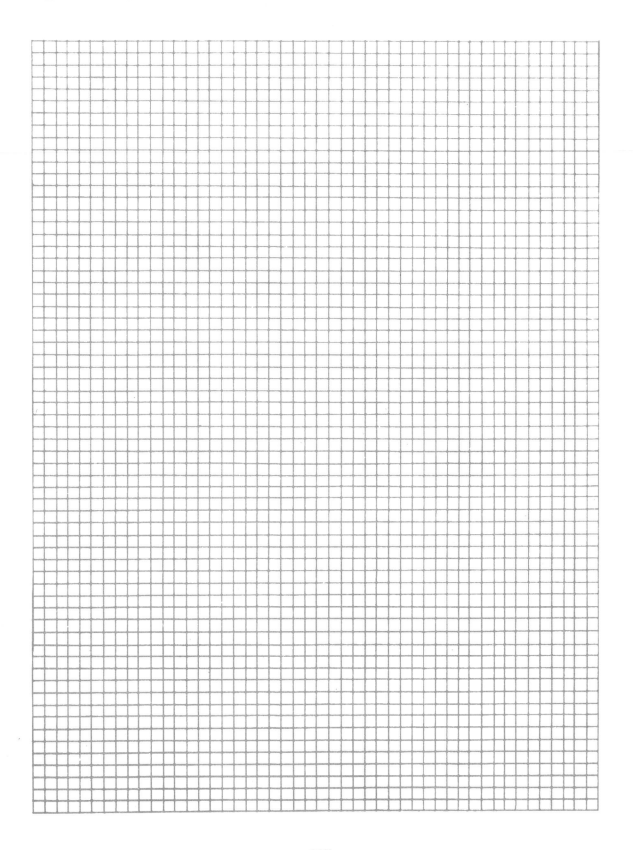

Unit 45   LEAD SHOWER PAN OR SAFE

RELATED INFORMATION

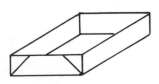

Sheet lead work is part of the plumbing trade. The lead sheets are fabricated into various shapes to fit the job. Some lead fabrications are self-supporting but many are a liner.

Sheet lead is described by the weight per square foot. Five pound lead sheet weighs 5 pounds per square foot. It is also 5/64 of an inch thick as a square foot of lead weighs one pound for each 64th of an inch of thickness.

SAMPLE PROBLEM

A lead shower pan is to have a floor size of 30″ × 36″. The pan is to be 6″ deep.

   a. Make a dimensioned sketch of the completed shower pan.

   b. Make a stretchout sketch of the layout on flat lead sheet.
Use envelope corners.

   c. Compute the area of the stretchout.

   d. Compute the weight of lead used if made of 3 lb. lead sheet.

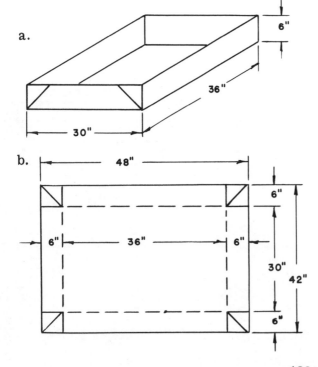

c. $A = LW$

$$A = \frac{48}{12} \times \frac{42}{12}$$

$A = 4' \times 3.5'$

$A = 14.0$ sq. ft.   <u>Ans.</u>

d. 14 sq. ft.
  × 3 lbs./sq. ft.
    42 lbs. of lead   <u>Ans.</u>

ASSIGNMENT

For each shower pan size listed:

a. Draw a dimensional sketch of completed pan.

b. Draw a dimensional stretchout sketch.

c. Compute the area of the stretchout.

d. Compute the total weight of the lead sheet using the thickness given.

1. Floor Size - 40″ × 32″   Depth - 4″   Lead Sheet - 5 lbs./sq. ft.

c. _____

d. _____

2. Floor Size - 35″ × 34″   Depth - 5″   Lead Sheet - 3/64″ thick

c. _____

d. _____

3. Floor Size - 36″ × 36″   Depth - 5″   Lead Sheet - 7 lbs./sq.ft.

c. _____

d. _____

4. Floor Size - 32″ × 43″   Depth - 6″   Lead Sheet - 3 lbs./sq.ft.

c. _____

d. _____

Unit 46   RECTANGULAR TANK LINER

RELATED INFORMATION

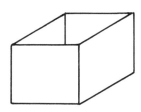

The rectangular tank liner might be for a chemical laboratory sink or an industrial tank. It differs from the shower pan in that it is not practical to use the envelope corner. Since the corner material is cut away, the corner seams are soldered or lead-burned.   For best corrosion resistance, lead-burning is required. It requires someone with this special skill to do the work.

SAMPLE PROBLEM

A tank 30″ wide by 50″ long and 24″ deep is to have a liner of 7 lb. lead sheet.

a. Draw a dimensioned sketch of the completed liner.

b. Draw a dimensioned stretchout sketch of the liner.

c. Compute the square feet of a lead sheet used.

d. Compute the weight of lead used.

a.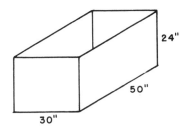

b.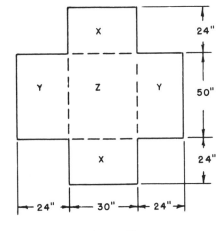

c. Area X

$$A = LW$$
$$A = \frac{30}{12} \times \frac{24}{12}$$
$$A = 2.5 \times 2$$
$$A = 5 \text{ sq. ft.}$$

Area Y

$$A = LW$$
$$A = \frac{50}{12} \times \frac{24}{12}$$
$$A = \frac{25}{6} \times 2$$
$$A = 8.33 \text{ sq. ft.}$$

Area Z

$$A = LW$$
$$A = \frac{50}{12} \times \frac{30}{12}$$
$$A = \frac{25}{6} \times \frac{5}{2} = \frac{125}{12}$$
$$A = 10.41 \text{ sq. ft.}$$

Total area = 2X + 2Y + Z
= 10. + 16.66 + 10.41
= 37.07 sq. ft. <u>Ans.</u>

d. Weight = 37.07 × 7 = 259.49 lbs.   <u>Ans.</u>

ASSIGNMENT

For each tank and sheet lead given:

a. Make a dimensioned sketch of the completed liner for the tank.

b. Make a dimensioned stretchout sketch of the liner.

c. Compute the square feet of sheet lead used.

d. Compute the weight of the lead used.

1. Tank Size - 40″ × 20″ × 20″ deep   Lead Sheet - 5/64″ thick

c. _____

d. _____

2. Tank Size - 22″ × 16″ × 11″ deep   Lead Sheet - 1/16″ thick

c. _____

d. _____

3. Tank Size - 3′-6″ × 2′-9″ × 3′-0″ deep   Lead Sheet - 3 lbs./sq. ft.

c. _____

d. _____

4. Tank Size - 18″ × 14″ × 10″ deep   Lead Sheet - 5 lbs./sq. ft.

c. _____

d. _____

RELATED INFORMATION

A lead tube or cylinder is made by wrapping a rectangular piece of sheet lead into a cylindrical shape. The ends are butted together and soldered or lead-burned. Roof flanges and round pans or liners require the tube construction.

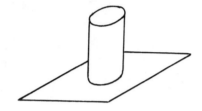

The roof flange consists of a tube and a plate. It is used to make a watertight connection between a vent stack and the roof. In good construction the tube is of sufficient length to be turned into the end of the vent pipe to make a raintight connection between the pipe and the roof flange. The plate is large enough to allow a watertight joint between it and the roofing. Roofing cement is used to seal this connection on a flat roof.

SAMPLE PROBLEM

A roof flange for a flat roof has a tube, 5″ diameter and 22″ high.   The plate is 18″ × 18″. Both are made of 5 lb. sheet lead.

- a. Make a dimensioned sketch of the completed roof flange.
- b. Make a dimensioned stretchout of the tube.
- c. Make a dimensioned stretchout of the plate.
- d. Compute the square feet of lead sheet used.
- e. Compute the weight of the lead sheet used.

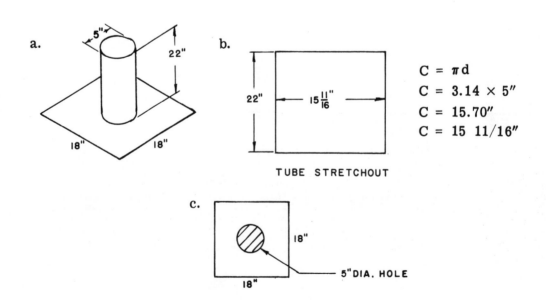

$$C = \pi d$$
$$C = 3.14 \times 5''$$
$$C = 15.70''$$
$$C = 15\ 11/16''$$

TUBE STRETCHOUT

d. Tube

$A = LW$

$A = \dfrac{22}{12} \times \dfrac{15.7}{12}$

$A = \dfrac{11}{6} \times \dfrac{15.7}{12}$

$A = 2.39$ sq. ft.

Plate

$A = S^2 - \pi R^2$

$A = 18'' \times 18'' - (3.14 \times 2.5'' \times 2.5'')$

$A = 324$ sq. in.. $- 19.625$ sq. in.

$A = 304.375$ sq. in.

$A = 2.11$ sq. ft.

Total areas = 2.39 sq. ft. + 2.11 sq. ft. = 4.5 sq. ft.   Ans.

e. Weight = 4.5 sq. ft. $\times$ 5 = 22.5 lbs.   Ans.

ASSIGNMENT

For each problem

   a. Make a dimensioned sketch of the completed job.

   b. Make a dimensioned stretchout of the tube.

   c. Make a dimensioned stretchout of the plate or bottom.

   d. Compute the square feet of lead sheet used.

   e. Compute the weight of the lead sheet used.

1. Job - Roof flange with 6" diam. tube   Lead Sheet - 3 lbs./sq. ft.
   20" high and 18" $\times$ 18" plate

d. _____   e. _____

2. Job - Roof flange 8 1/2″ diam. tube　　　Lead Sheet - 5 lbs./sq. ft.
        24″ high with 24″ × 24″ plate

d. _____　　　　　e. _____

3. Job - Circular shower pan　　　　　Lead Sheet - 5 lbs./sq. ft.
        40″ diam., 6″ high

d. _____　　　　　e. _____

RELATED INFORMATION

Roof pitch is a method of dimensioning the angle or steepness of a roof. Since most roofs are of gable style, pitch is determined from the rise and span of a double slope or isosceles triangle.

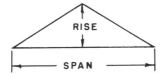

Pitch $= \dfrac{\text{rise}}{\text{span}}$

Rise = pitch × span

Thus, a house with 5' rise and 15' span would be 1/3 pitch.

The full size of the roof would be difficult to work with for layout of a roof flange or other construction work. For layout a standard span of 24" is used. By using only one slope, thus a standard run of 12", a right triangle is obtained. For 1/3 pitch the rise is 1/3 × 24" or 8". The run is 12".

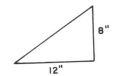

A right triangle of 12" base and 8" altitude is exactly 1/3 pitch.

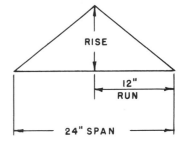

SAMPLE PROBLEM

A 6" O. D. lead tube is to be made into a 1/3 pitch roof flange.

a. How can the angle at the bottom of the tube be dimensioned?

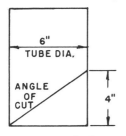

Since there would be 8" rise for 12" of run, for 6" of run the rise is 6/12 × 8" or <u>4"</u>   **Ans.**

b. What size hole must be cut in the plate?

Construct a right triangle with 6" base and 4" rise. Measure the slope; it will be approximately 7 1/4". The hole in the plate is an ellipse with major diameter of 7 1/4" and minor diameter of 6". <u>Ans.</u>

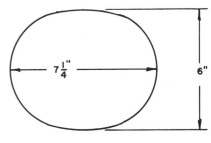

OPENING IN PLATE

ASSIGNMENT

For each problem

a. Compute the rise for 24″ of span.

b. Determine the altitude to use to obtain the proper angle on the tube for a roof flange.

c. Make a dimensioned sketch of the hole through the plate.

1. Pitch 1/3   Tube - 3″ diameter

a. _____

b. _____

2. Pitch 1/4   Tube - 4″ diameter

a. _____

b. _____

3. Pitch 1/2   Tube - 5″ diameter

a. _____

b. _____

4. Pitch 1/8   Tube - 6″ diameter

a. _____

b. _____

Section IV VOLUMES, PRESSURE, CAPACITIES

Unit 49   WATER MEASURE

RELATED INFORMATION

Volumes are often computed in cubic inches for smaller quantities. The U. S. Bureau of Standards has set 231 cu. in. as a U. S. gallon. Thus, cu. in. ÷ 231 = gallons.

Larger volumes are computed in cubic feet. There are nearly 7.5 gallons in one cubic foot. So cubic feet × 7.5 = gallons.

Water weighs nearly 62.5 lbs. for a cubic foot or 8.33 lbs. for a gallon.

Cu. ft. × 62.5 = lbs. of water or Gals. × 8.33 = lbs. of water

SAMPLE PROBLEMS

1. A tank has a volume of 1000 cu. in.

   a. How many gallons volume?   1000 ÷ 231 = 4.32 gals.   Ans.

   b. What weight of water can it hold?   4.32 gals. × 8.33 = 35.9856
                                            or 35.99 lbs. Ans.

2. A tank has a capacity of 80 cu. ft.

   a. How many pounds of water can it hold?   62.5 × 80 = 5000 lbs.   Ans.

   b. How many gallons of water can it hold?   7.5 × 80 = 600 gals.   Ans.

ASSIGNMENT

For each volume compute (a) the gallons, (b) the weight of water that could be held.

	Volume	Gallons	Weight
1.	1600 cu. in.		
2.	5000 cu. in.		
3.	18 cu. ft.		
4.	275 cu. ft.		
5.	115.75 cu. ft.		

Unit 50   RECTANGULAR SOLIDS

RELATED INFORMATION

Volume is always calculated from three dimensions multiplied together. The rectangular shape may be a tank, a swimming pool, a ditch and other trade applications.

In order to obtain an answer in cubic inches, multiply inches × inches × inches. For cubic feet multiply feet × feet × feet. Earth and concrete volumes are usually in cubic yards. They are calculated as cubic feet and changed to cubic yards by dividing by 27.

SAMPLE PROBLEMS

1. A flush tank is 21″ × 6 1/2″ and has water to a depth of 13″. How many cubic inches of water does it contain? How many gallons?

    $V = LWH$

    $V = 21″ × 6.5″ × 13″$

    $V = 1774.5$ cu. in.   <u>Ans.</u>

    $V = 1774.5 ÷ 231 = 7.68$ gallons   <u>Ans.</u>

2. A flat roof 25′ × 46′ is 2″ deep with water. How many cu. ft. of water does it contain? How much does the water weigh?

    $V = LWH$

    $V = 25′ × 46′ × \dfrac{2}{12}$

    $V = 25′ × 46′ × \dfrac{1}{6}$

    $V = 191 \ 2/3$ cu. ft.   <u>Ans.</u>   Weight = $191.67 × 62.5 =$
    11979.375 lbs.   <u>Ans.</u>

3. A pipe trench is 60′ long, 2′-6″ wide and an average depth of 4′-9″. How many cu. yds. were removed?

    $V = LWH$

    $V = 60′ × 2.5′ × 4.75′$

    $V = 712.50$ cu. ft.

    $V = 712.50 ÷ 27 = 26.38$ cu. yds.   <u>Ans.</u>

ASSIGNMENT

1. A flush tank is 19″ × 10 1/2″ and holds water to a depth of 11″. How many cu. in. of water does it hold? How many gallons?

   _____

   _____

2. A swimming pool is 22′ × 30′ with an average depth of 3′-3″. How many cu. ft. of water can it contain? How many gallons?

   _____

   _____

3. In digging a trench 50′-0″ long, 2′-3″ wide and 3′-6″ deep, how many cu. ft. of earth were removed? How many cu. yds.?

   _____

   _____

4. A flat roof 14′ × 23′ is 4″ deep with water. How many cu. ft. of water? How many gallons? How many pounds?

   _____

   _____

   _____

5. A rectangular metal tank with a capacity of 50 gallons has to be built in a space which allows a base dimension of 16″ × 20″. How high must the tank be built?

   _____

6. What is the capacity, in cu. ft., of the septic tank shown at the right?

   _____

   What is its capacity in gallons?
   (Cu. ft. × 7.5 = gallons)

   _____

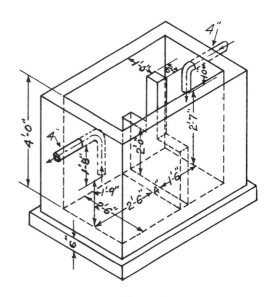

7. A septic tank holding 840 gals. is 7′ long and 4′ deep, inside measurements. What is its capacity, in cu. ft.?

   _____

   How wide should this tank be?

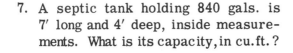

SEPTIC TANK

   _____

Unit 51   CYLINDERS

RELATED INFORMATION

The basic formula for the volume of a cylinder is $V = \pi r^2 h$, or $V = .7854\, d^2 h$. Both are somewhat long in the amount of multiplying required. Notice that there are three dimensions as in any volume. The constant adjusts the size of the answer for the shape of the cylinder. Use 3.14 as π with the radius or .7854 with the diameter.

A short-cut to get volumes of cylinders in gallons is $.0408\, d^2 h$ where d is measured in inches and h is measured in feet. This formula works because a cylinder 1 inch in diameter and 1 foot long holds .0408 gallons.

For standard weight pipe it is easy to look on a data sheet (see Data #21, Appendix) for the gallons held in one foot and multiply by the number of feet of pipe. In draining or filling a pipe line it is sometimes desirable to know how much water is held in the pipe.

SAMPLE PROBLEMS

1. A circular pool is 38″ in diameter and 15″ deep. Compute its volume in gallons.

$$V = \pi r^2 h$$

$$V = 3.14 \times 19'' \times 19'' \times 15''$$

$$V = 17003.1 \text{ cu. in.}$$

$$V = 17003.1 \div 231 = 73.6 \text{ gallons} \quad \underline{Ans.}$$

2. How many gallons will a range boiler 13″ in diameter and 5′ high hold?

$$V = .0408\, d^2 h$$

$$V = .0408 \times 13'' \times 13'' \times 5'$$

$$V = 34.476 \text{ gallons} \quad \underline{Ans.}$$

3. How many gallons of water can a 3″ standard weight pipe hold if it is 18′ long? (See Data #21, Appendix)

.384 gals. per lineal ft. $\times$ 18′ = 6.912 gals. $\quad$ <u>Ans.</u>

ASSIGNMENT

1. A water tank is 8'-0" in diameter and 12'-0" high. Compute its capacity in cubic feet and in gallons.

    _____

    _____

2. A gasoline storage tank is 42" in diameter and 40" high. Compute its volume in cubic inches and in gallons.

    _____

    _____

3. A range boiler is 16" in diameter and 4'-0" high. Compute its volume in gallons.

    _____

4. Compute the capacity of each of the following sizes and lengths of standard weight pipe.

    a. 2" pipe, 45'-0" long   _____

    b. 4" pipe, 28'-0" long   _____

    c. 10" pipe, 30'-0" long   _____

    d. 3/4" pipe, 120'-0" long   _____

5. Compute the weight of each pipe listed in Problem 4. See Data #21, Appendix.

    a. _____

    b. _____

    c. _____

    d. _____

6. Compute the weight of water that could be in each pipe listed in Problem 4.

    a. _____

    b. _____

    c. _____

    d. _____

Unit 52 SPHERES

RELATED INFORMATION

A sphere or half-sphere has nearly equal forces pushing in all directions when it is filled with water. Thus, the shape adds to the strength of the structure. Some tanks are built as spheres but more often a spherical bottom is used on a cylindrical tank.

The formula of a sphere is given in several slightly different forms in handbooks.

$V = .5236 d^3$ is a convenient way of writing the formula. For a half-sphere use one-half the volume of a whole sphere or

$$\frac{.5236\ d^3}{2}$$

SAMPLE PROBLEM

A sphere has a diameter of 9″. Compute its volume in cu. in.

$$V = .5236 d^3$$

$$V = .5236 \times 9'' \times 9'' \times 9''$$

$$V = 381.7044 \text{ cu. in.} \quad \underline{\text{Ans.}}$$

What is the volume of a half-sphere 9″ in diameter?

$$V = \frac{381.70}{2}$$

$$V = 190.85 \text{ cu. in.} \quad \underline{\text{Ans.}}$$

ASSIGNMENT

1. A marble top lavatory has a semi-spherical porcelain bowl with an inside radius of 7″. How much water, in cu. in., will the bowl hold?

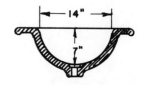

2. How many gallons of water does the circular water tower contain, as shown in the sketch?

_____

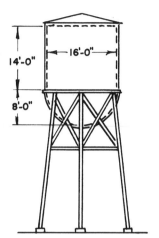

3. What is the pressure per square inch at the base of a standpipe terminating 30 ft. below the tank bottom if the tank shown right is filled?

(Pressure is 0.434 per sq. in. per foot of height.)

_____

4. A spherical gas tank has an inside diameter of 14 ft. Compute the number of cubic feet of gas in the tank when it is full.   _____

5. If the spherical gas tank had an inside radius of 6'-6" and were half-full, how many cubic feet of gas would it contain?   _____

6. Which of the following has the greater capacity and how much greater: a spherical gas chamber with inside diameter of 11 ft. or a cylindrical-shaped chamber with 10 ft. inside diameter and 10 ft. height?   _____

_____

Unit 53   SEGMENTS

RELATED INFORMATION

Some cylindrical tanks are installed on the side instead of standing on end. When such a tank is partly filled there is a segment volume calculation. The volume is equal to the area of the end times the length of the tank.

The simplest formula for finding the approximate area of a segment is:

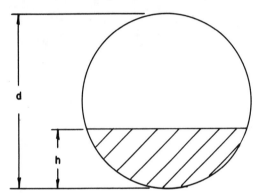

$$A = \frac{4h^2}{3} \sqrt{\frac{d}{h} - .608} \text{ when } A = \text{area}$$

$$d = \text{diameter}$$

$$h = \text{height of segment}$$

SAMPLE PROBLEM

a. Compute the cu. in. volume in tank shown below.

b. Convert this volume to gallons.

$$A = \frac{4h^2}{3} \sqrt{\frac{d}{h} - .608}$$

$$A = \frac{4}{3} \times 144 \sqrt{\frac{18}{12} - .608}$$

$$A = \frac{576}{3} \sqrt{1.5 - .608}$$

$$A = 192 \sqrt{.892}$$

$$A = 192 \times .94$$

$$A = 180.48 \text{ sq. in.}$$

$$V = AL$$

$$V = 180.48 \times 22$$

$$V = 3970.56 \text{ cu. in.} \quad \underline{\text{Ans.}}$$

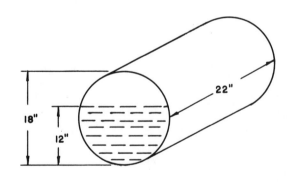

$$\text{Gallons} = \frac{3970.56}{231} = 17.18 \text{ gals.} \quad \underline{\text{Ans.}}$$

ASSIGNMENT

1. What is the area of a segment of a circle whose diameter is
   42″, and the height of the segment is 14″?   _____

2. Find the number of cubic feet of steam space in the gas tube
   boiler, as shown in the sketch below. The boiler is 18′ long
   between heads, has an inside diameter of 66″, and the mean
   water line is 20″ from the top.   _____

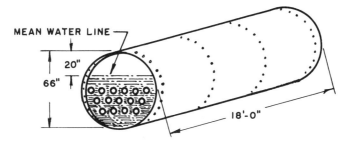

MEAN WATER LINE

20″

66″

18′-0″

3. A pneumatic water system has a tank 25′ long and a 4 1/2′
   inside diameter which is set in a horizontal position. If this
   tank is filled to a level equal to 2/3 of its diameter, how many
   gallons of water does it contain?   _____

4. An oil tank, which is 12′ long and 4′ in diameter inside
   measurements, is placed in a horizontal position. See the
   drawing below. Make up a table showing
   how much oil there will be in the
   tank for each of the levels.

48″
42″
36″
30″
4′-0″ 24″
18″
12″
6″

12′-0″

Measuring Pole	Gallons
6″	
12″	
18″	
24″	
30″	
36″	
42″	
48″	

Unit 54   WATER PRESSURE, HEAD, AND FORCE

RELATED INFORMATION

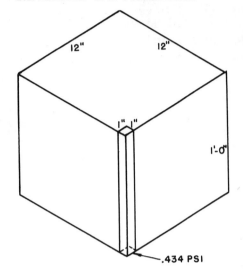

In plumbing practice, water pressure is measured by a gage or by the height or "head". The pressure gage measures in pounds per square inch. Head is measured in feet.

To determine how high a pressure tank can lift water, it is necessary to convert pounds per square inch to feet of head. When a waste and vent stack is tested by being filled with water, the head can be changed to pounds per square inch. The total force against a test plug is the area times the pressure.

The pressure per sq. in. of water, per foot of height, equals

$$\frac{62.5 \text{ lbs. (weight of 1 cu. ft. water)}}{144 \text{ (sq. in. or 1 sq. ft.)}} = .434 \text{ lb. per sq. in.}$$

$$\frac{1.000}{.434} = 2.304 \text{ ft.} = 27.648 \text{ in.} - \text{ the height or head necessary to produce 1 lb. pressure per square inch}$$

PSI = .434 × H where PSI = pressure per sq. in. and H = height of water in ft.

● Each and every foot of head (or height) produces .434 lb. pressure per square inch.

● Each and every pound per square inch of pressure requires a head of 2.304 feet.

● The shape or slope of the sides of a tank do not affect the pressure on the bottom of a tank.

SAMPLE PROBLEMS

1. A stack 42' high above a test plug is filled with water. Compute the pounds per square inch (PSI) on the test plug.

.434 × 42' = 18.228 PSI   <u>Ans.</u>

148

2. How high will 25 PSI lift water?

$$2.304' \times 25 = 57.600 \text{ feet} \quad \underline{\text{Ans.}}$$

3. Compute the total force on a 6" diameter test plug with a water head of 15'.

$$.434 \times 15' = 6.5100 \text{ PSI} \quad A = \pi r^2 \qquad\qquad 28.26 \times 6.51 = 183.9726 \text{ lbs.}$$
$$= 3.14 \times 3'' \times 3'' \qquad\qquad\qquad \underline{\text{Ans.}}$$
$$= 28.26 \text{ sq. in.}$$

ASSIGNMENT

1. What will be the pressure, in pounds per square inch, on the base of a 4" soil stack 45 feet high that is filled with water? _____

2. What would be the height, in feet, of a column of water necessary to develop 13.02 lbs. pressure per square inch? _____

3. What head of water will produce a 65 lb. pressure per square inch? 72 lbs. per square inch? 88 lbs. per square inch? _____   _____   _____

4. What pressure is produced by a 28 ft. head? A 49 1/2 ft. head? A 67 1/2 ft. head? _____   _____   _____

5. Determine the pounds of force on a 4" diameter test plug in a stack with a head of 20 feet. _____

6. Determine the pounds of force on a 3" diameter test plug in a stack with a head of 48 feet. _____

Unit 55   RATIO OF PIPE CAPACITIES

RELATED INFORMATION

Pressure, friction and cross-sectional area of the pipes control the amount of flow in piping. Water pressure is beyond the control of the plumber in most installations. Friction is somewhat reduced by proper design of a piping system to run as directly as possible. The material used may also affect friction as copper tubing has a smoother wall than steel or wrought iron pipe. The smoother surface has less frictional resistance.

Adequate size pipe is the best solution to provide adequate flow to each faucet. Only in a fire sprinkler system must all outlets have full flow at the same time. In plumbing a per cent of full use is expected. The architect would be expected to determine the number of outlets in use at one time.

There are two ways of computing the ratio of pipe capacities. The first, $\frac{D^2}{d^2}$, is a simplification of AREA ÷ area and makes no allowance for friction. It is simple to use and gives a usable answer when the large diameter is not more than twice the small diameter.

A more accurate comparison is obtained by $\sqrt{\left(\frac{D}{d}\right)^5}$ which does allow for friction. Friction is greater in smaller pipes because a greater percentage of the total water drags against the pipe wall.

SAMPLE PROBLEMS

1. How many 1" pipes can be supplied by a 2" pipe?

$$R = \frac{D^2}{d^2} \quad \text{where} \quad \begin{aligned} R &= \text{number of smaller pipes} \\ D &= \text{diameter of larger pipe} \\ d &= \text{diameter of smaller pipes} \end{aligned}$$

$$R = \frac{4}{1} = 4 \quad \underline{\text{Ans.}}$$

2. How many 3/4" pipes can be supplied by a 1" pipe?

$$R = \frac{D^2}{d^2}$$

$$R = \frac{1 \times 1}{.75 \times .75} = \frac{1}{.5625}$$

$$R = 1.7 \text{ or about } 2 \quad \underline{\text{Ans.}}$$

3. How many 2" pipes will a 4" pipe supply, allowing for friction?

$$R \text{ varies as } \sqrt{\left(\frac{D}{d}\right)^5}$$

R = number of smaller pipes the larger one will supply

D = diameter of larger pipe

d = diameter of smaller pipes

$$R = \sqrt{\left(\frac{4}{2}\right)^5} = \sqrt{(2)^5} = \sqrt{32} = 5.657 \quad \underline{Ans.}$$

ASSIGNMENT

Solve each problem using both formulas.

	$\frac{D^2}{d^2}$	$\sqrt{\left(\frac{D}{d}\right)^5}$
1. How many 2" pipes will a 3" pipe supply?	_____	_____
2. How many 3/4" pipes will a 2" pipe supply?	_____	_____
3. How many 1 1/4" pipes will a 3 1/2" pipe supply?	_____	_____
4. How many 1/2" pipes will a 1 1/4" pipe supply?	_____	_____
5. How many 1" pipes will a 1 1/2" pipe supply?	_____	_____

Section V HEATING

Unit 56   HEAT LOSS VS. RADIATOR SIZE

RELATED INFORMATION

Radiator and boiler sizes for heating are not too difficult to compute. The principle is to balance the heat loss with the heat supply. While the principle and type of calculation are easily understood, the variations are many. These units on heating will illustrate the method based on a one-pipe steam system using the usual type column-radiators without enclosures. A study such as this should provide basic information and a starting point for other radiation systems.

Manufacturers and distributors of heating equipment have detailed information for heat calculation. They will supply information and even the services of a heating expert for most installations. The calculation of radiation requires specific information. To know how the calculations are made is an aid to supplying the necessary data about the building to be heated.

The unit of heat is the British Thermal Unit, (BTU). It is the amount of heat that can raise the temperature of one pound of water one degree Fahrenheit.

Heat is lost from a room through any area exposed to a lower temperature. It is also lost by the heating of incoming air due to infiltration and for ventilation. Table 1 on the following page shows the heat loss per square foot per hour for one degree of temperature difference. Table 2 shows infiltration heat loss per cubic foot per hour for each degree temperature difference.

Different materials and different types of construction vary in the rate of heat loss. The steam radiator will supply 240 BTU per hour for each square foot of radiator surface. In comparison the same radiator in a hot water system will give off 150 BTU per hour.

SAMPLE PROBLEMS

1. How much heat would be lost through a window 3'-0" × 4'-0" if the temperature is 70° inside and 0° outside?

    Heat loss = constant × temperature difference × area

    Heat loss = 1.13 (see Table) × 70 × 12

    Heat loss = 949.2 BTU   <u>Ans.</u>

2. How much steam radiation would offset the heat loss in Problem 1?
    949.2 ÷ 240 = 3.95 square feet of radiation   <u>Ans.</u>

TABLE 1 - HEAT LOSS PER SQUARE FOOT PER HOUR

BTU Heat Loss for Various Standard Constructions -
Walls, Ceilings and Windows

WALL CONSTRUCTION	BTU PER DEGREE FAHRENHEIT		
	No Insulation	1/2″ Rigid	3 5/8″ Batt
Frame - Siding or shingles, building paper, sheathing, plaster or wall board	.26	.20	.10
Frame - Brick veneer, building paper, sheathing, plaster or wall board	.28	.21	.10
8″ brick - 1″ furring, lath and plaster	.32	.22	
8″ hollow tile or cinder block, 1″ stucco finish	.37		
4″ brick and 8″ tile or cinder block	.34		
12″ concrete, plain	.57		
CEILING CONSTRUCTION			
Ceiling - lath and plastered Floored on joists	.25	.10	.07
Ceiling - lath and plastered Unfloored	.70	.26	.10

WINDOWS AND DOORS

Single glass - 1.13   With storm windows - .75

Double glass with sealed space between   - .65

Doors, with or without glass, same as windows

Glass block, 3 7/8″ thick -   .49

TABLE 2 - HEAT LOSS PER CUBIC FOOT PER HOUR

BTU Heat Loss to Incoming Air by Infiltration for Various
Window Construction and Walls Exposed

EXPOSURE	WEATHER STRIP OR STORM SASH	
	No	Yes
An outside wall of room	.018	.009
Two walls	.027	.014
Three walls	.036	.018
Entrance halls	.036	.018
Sun Rooms	.054	.027

ASSIGNMENT

For each of the following, compute the heat loss and the square feet of steam radiation to supply heat equal to the loss.

1. A single glass window 3'-6" × 4'-0" with temperature of 75° inside and 0° outside.

2. A double glass (storm window) 2'-9" × 4'-6" with 70° inside and 0° outside.

3. A ceiling, no insulation, 20'-0" × 12'-6" with 70° temperature difference.

4. A ceiling with 3 5/8" of rock wool, 32'-0" × 14'-9", with 70° temperature difference.

5. A 12" thick plain concrete wall, no openings, 18'-0" × 8'-0", with 70° inside and 10° outside.

Unit 57 RADIATOR SIZE FOR TOTAL HEAT LOSS OF A ROOM

RELATED INFORMATION

A single radiator is large enough to equal several heat losses in a room. The usual heat losses are through walls, through windows and doors, and in heating cold air either for ventilation or because of infiltration. The ceiling is another source of heat loss unless there is a heated room above.

Since most houses have all the rooms heated it will be necessary to only include outside walls in the total wall area. The sample problem shows the method for grouping heat losses in a room.

SAMPLE PROBLEM

Compute the heat loss and the steam radiator size for the dining room in the one floor house. See Floor Plan, Figure 1. The walls are standard frame construction. There are no storm windows. The ceiling is insulated with 3 5/8" of rock wool. The temperature difference is 70°.

Room name - <u>DINING ROOM</u>   Room dimensions - <u>11'-2" X 11'-2" X 8'-0"</u>

		Coefficient	BTU Loss
Volume cubic feet	999.36	X .027 X 70	1883
Total wall area	178.56		
Less: Glass and door areas	22.5	X 1.13 X 70	1750
Net wall area	156.06	X .26 X 70	2839
Square feet of ceiling	124.54	X .10 X 70	871
Miscellaneous			
Total			7343

Square feet of radiation -   7343 ÷ 240 = 30.6   **Ans.**

ASSIGNMENT

For each room follow the procedures as in the Sample Problem. Compute the heat loss and the steam radiator size for each of the following locations in the one floor house. Use the same specifications as for the Sample Problem.

1. Living room
2. Bedroom No. 1 with closet
3. Bedroom No. 2 with closet
4. Bath, allowing 10% extra for higher temperature
5. Kitchen
6. Entry

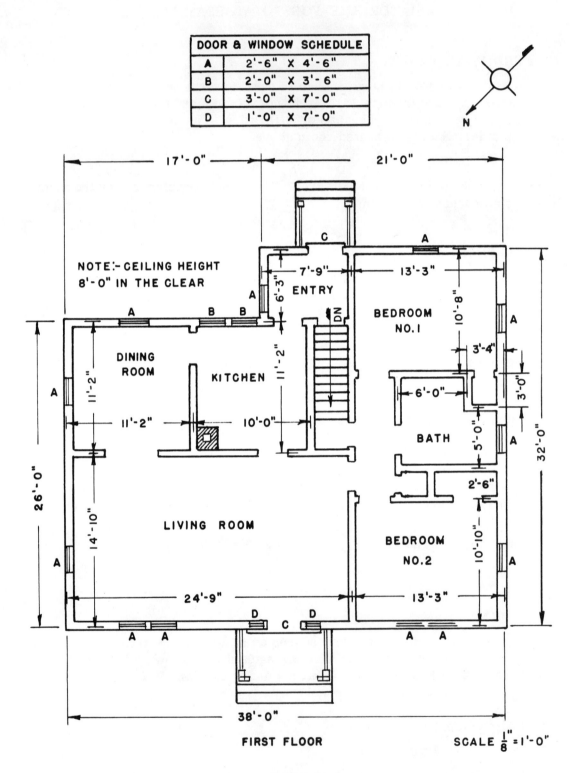

DOOR & WINDOW SCHEDULE

A	2'-6" X 4'-6"
B	2'-0" X 3'-6"
C	3'-0" X 7'-0"
D	1'-0" X 7'-0"

NOTE:- CEILING HEIGHT
8'-0" IN THE CLEAR

FIRST FLOOR   SCALE $\frac{1}{8}$" = 1'-0"

FIG. I FLOOR PLAN

1. Living Room

2. Bedroom No. 1, with Closet

3. Bedroom No. 2, with Closet

4. Bath (Allow 10% Extra)

5. Kitchen

6. Entry

Unit 58   ESTIMATING SIZE OF PIPING

RELATED INFORMATION

The one pipe up-feed system consists of a single circuit main which rises from the boiler close to the basement ceiling and then grades down uniformly to permit flow of condensation.

Radiators have one connection through which the steam and the water of condensation flow in opposite directions.

After the last radiator in the line has been served, the main is dripped just beyond the branch of connection and a smaller return line is installed which carries the water or condensation back to the boiler. This return may be below the boiler water line, and called a "wet return", or it may be above the water line, in which case it is called a "dry return."

In the one pipe up-feed system the pressure must be kept nearly equal in all parts; otherwise, the water will not be able to return to the boiler and will remain in the radiators and piping.

In no other system is the sizing of the piping as important as in the one pipe system.

Tables showing sizes of pipe to use in working out the problems attached are shown below.

TABLE NO. 1
RADIATOR CONNECTIONS

Size of Pipe	Sq. Ft. of Radiation
1″	24 or less
1 1/4″	25 - 60
1 1/2″	61 - 120
2″	121 - 300

TABLE NO. 2
RISER AND RUNOUT CONNECTIONS

Sq. Ft. of Radiation	Risers	Runouts
25 or less	1″	1 1/4″
26 - 60	1 1/4″	1 1/2″
61 - 150	1 1/2″	2″
151 - 350	2″	2 1/2″
351 - 600	2 1/2″	3″
601 - 900	3″	3 1/2″

TABLE NO. 3

SIZE OF STEAM MAINS AND RETURNS BASED UPON EXPERIENCE

Sq. Ft. of Radiation	Steam Main	Wet Return	Dry Return
300 or less	2″	1″	1 1/2″
301 – 600	2 1/2″	1″	1 1/2″
601 – 900	3″	1 1/4″	1 1/2″
901 – 1600	4″	1 1/4″	2″
1601 – 2500	5″	1 1/2″	2″
2501 – 3600	6″	1 1/2″	2 1/2″

ASSIGNMENT

Figure 1 below shows the layout for a complete steam job, showing the amount of radiation in each room together with the lengths of mains. The distance between floors is 10 feet.

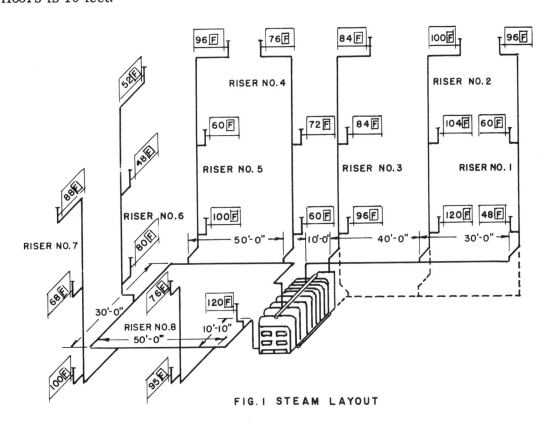

FIG. I STEAM LAYOUT

Using Fig. 1, complete the tables which follow for

1. Radiator connections   3. Sizes of runouts

2. Sizes of risers   4. Sizes of steam mains

1. Radiator Connections

Riser No. (Sq. Ft.)	Floor	Capac- ity (Sq. Ft.)	Radiator Connec. Ans.	Floor	Capac- ity (Sq. Ft.)	Radiator Connec. Ans.	Floor	Capac- ity (Sq. Ft.)	Radiator Connec. Ans.

2. Sizes of Risers   3. Runouts   4. Sizes of Steam Mains

Capacity	To 1st Floor	To 2nd Floor	To 3rd Floor	Riser Runouts	Size	

5. What size boiler is needed for this job allowing 60% increase in excess of actual radiation? _____

6. On the Floor Plan, Figure 2, show next to each radiator the following information:

    a. The square feet of radiation from your calculations of the previous unit.

    b. The proper radiator connection size.

    c. The runout pipe size.

    d. The riser pipe size.

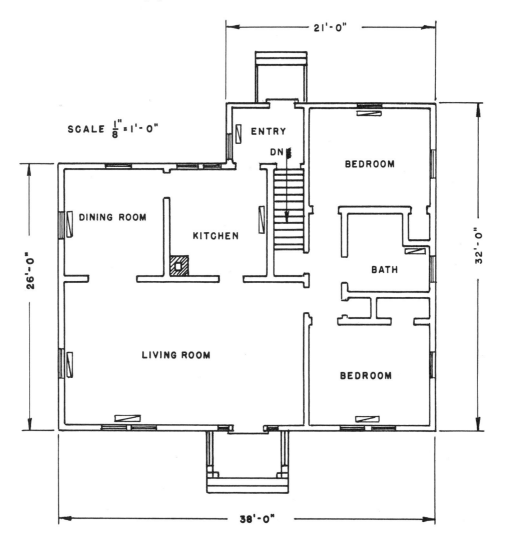

FIG. 2   FIRST FLOOR PLAN-RADIATOR LOCATIONS

7. On the basement plan, Figure 3, show the steam main pipe sizes and the pipe size for a wet return.

8. What BTU output size boiler will be needed if the boiler is to have a rating 40% higher than the total of all radiator capacity. _____

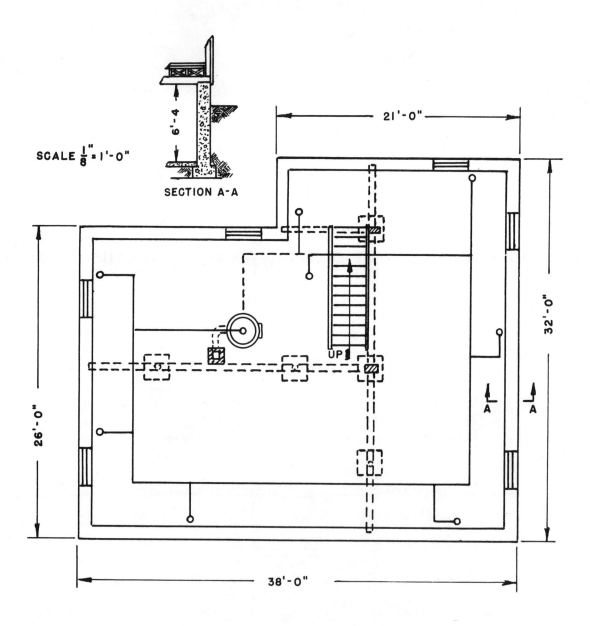

FIG. 3 BASEMENT PLAN

RELATED INFORMATION

The two floor plan house offers some differences in computing radiator sizes compared to the one floor house. The downstairs rooms do not have a heat loss through the ceilings as the upstairs is also heated. However, any first floor room with an unheated room above must include ceiling heat loss. This is also true for any room that is part of a one story section of a two story house. Thus in computing heat loss for a two story house it is necessary to examine both first and second story floor plans.

A partition between a room and an unfinished space should be computed as an outside wall. This is also true of a partition between heated rooms and an unheated storage room. Closets should be included in the heat loss for the room into which they open.

The heat for a basement comes from heat given off by steam piping and the boiler in the basement. This includes heat for the cellar stair space. Basement heat is one of the reasons for oversizing the boiler.

A stair space to the second floor must receive heat from adjacent rooms as it has no radiator of its own. For the two floor plan of the Assignment add the heat loss for the stair space to the kitchen heat loss.

ASSIGNMENT

The two floor house shown in the following plans has no insulation in walls or ceilings. All windows have storm windows and there are storm doors. The house is frame and there is no attic flooring.

1. List the first floor rooms with a heat loss through the ceiling.

    _____

    _____

2. Compute the heat loss and steam radiator size for each room. See Figures 2 and 4 for radiator locations. Only the storeroom is unheated.

    _____

    _____

    _____

    _____

    _____

163

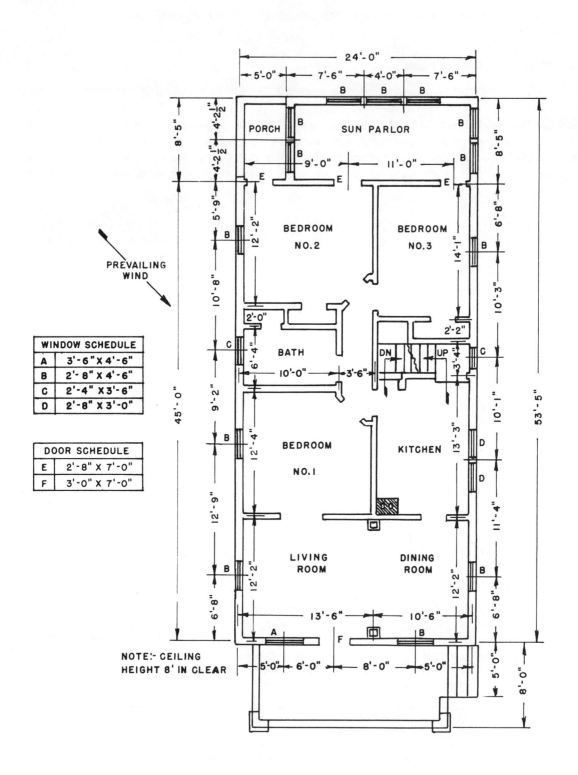

FIG. I FIRST FLOOR PLAN

164

3. On Figure 2, list next to each radiator:

   a. The size connection to the radiator.

   b. The runout size.

   c. The riser size.

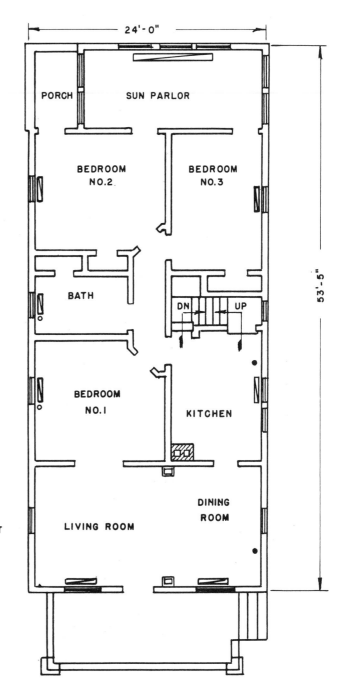

NOTE: CEILING HEIGHT
8'-0" IN CLEAR

FIG. 2
FIRST FLOOR PLAN
RADIATOR LOCATIONS

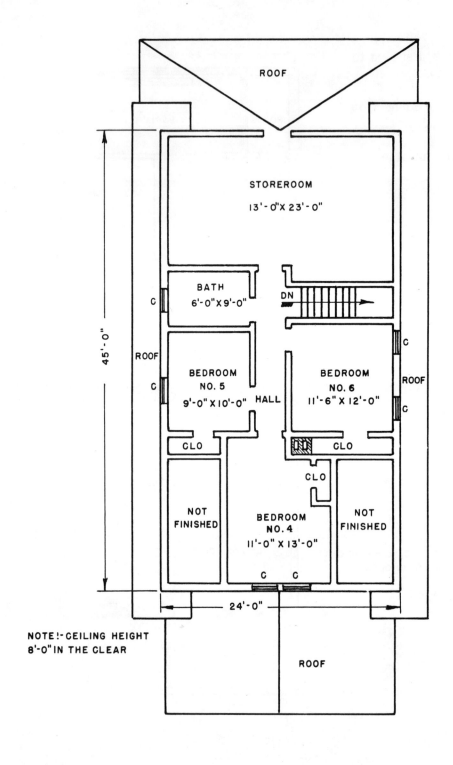

FIG 3 SECOND FLOOR PLAN

4. On Figure 4, list next to each radiator:

    a. The size connection to the radiator.

    b. The runout size.

    c. The riser size.

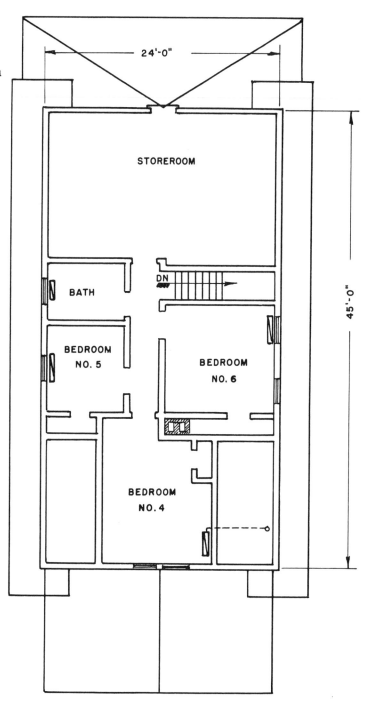

FIG. 4
SECOND FLOOR PLAN
RADIATOR LOCATIONS

5. On Fig. 5 show the proper
   steam main size starting
   at the boiler and following
   around to the wet returns,
   also showing wet return
   sizes.

6. What BTU capacity boiler
   would be used if the output
   rating is 40% more than
   total radiator capacity?

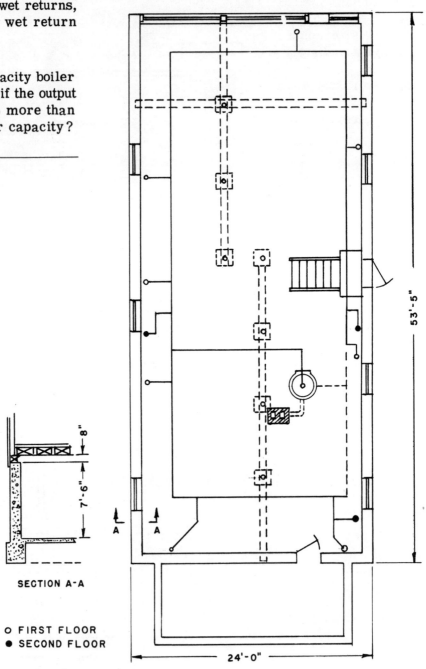

SECTION A-A

o FIRST FLOOR
● SECOND FLOOR

FIG. 5
BASEMENT PLAN

Section VI THE BUILDERS LEVEL

Unit 60 WORD USE IN LEVELING

RELATED INFORMATION

The builder's level is frequently used in the plumbing trade to determine elevations for pipe location. The instrument is a telescope supported on a tripod. The builder's level, when properly adjusted, gives the operator a level line of sight through the telescope. The telescope can be rotated to any direction. The instrument operator sights against a rod, which is a pole with measurements on it, held by another workman at chosen locations. The builder's level is a moderately expensive tool, but it "levels" in less time and more accurately than other methods. To work with this tool requires an understanding of terms and procedure.

1. The <u>Line of Sight</u> is an imaginary line through the telescope, centered on the cross hairs showing in lens and directed toward a measuring rod.

2. The <u>Instrument Location</u> is the place where the tripod is set up, usually about midpoint between stations.

3. A <u>Station</u> is the point where the rod man holds the rod. It is chosen with a purpose.

4. A <u>Bench mark</u> (B.M.) is a station of known elevation often established by others. The U.S. Coast and Geodetic Survey establishes bench marks with elevations above sea level. A construction site may have a bench mark located near the job, perhaps on the curb. For convenience the building bench mark may be listed at 100.00 feet elevation.

5. A <u>Turning Point</u> (T.P.) is a station located between instrument locations. It is used when a building or other obstacle prevents a direct line of sight.

6. The <u>Height of Instrument</u> (H.I.) is the elevation of the line of sight. It is the sum of the station elevation plus the back sight.

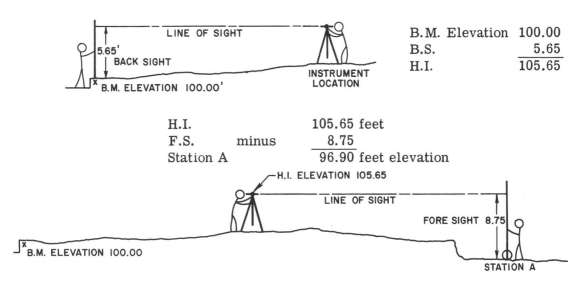

B.M. Elevation	100.00
B.S.	5.65
H.I.	105.65

H.I.		105.65 feet
F.S.	minus	8.75
Station A		96.90 feet elevation

169

7 A <u>Back Sight</u> (B.S.) is the measurement on the rod at the line of sight when the rod is held on a station of known elevation, as the bench mark. The back sight measurement is always added to the elevation to compute the height of the instrument.

8. A <u>Fore Sight</u> (F.S.) is the measurement on the rod at the line of sight when the rod is held on a station of unknown elevation. The station elevation is computed by subtracting the fore sight from the height of the instrument.

ASSIGNMENT

The profile and plot plan shows a leveling job to locate two top of manhole elevation stakes. The letters are to be matched to leveling terms in the table. For example, u and v are lines of sight and p + a is height of instrument.

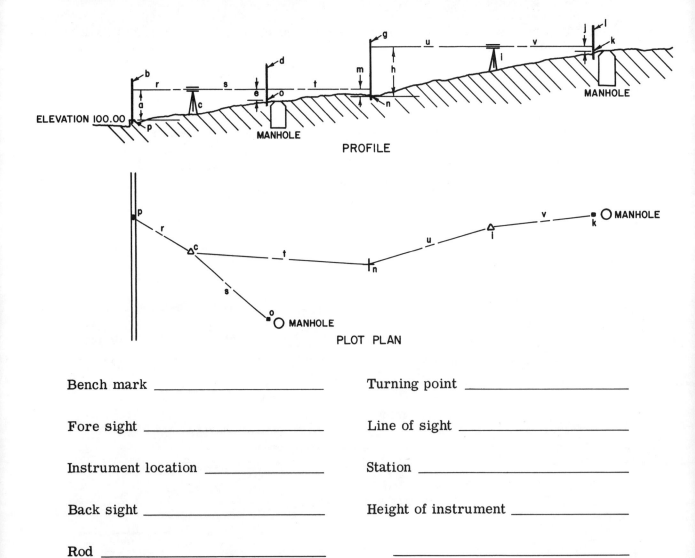

Bench mark _____

Fore sight _____

Instrument location _____

Back sight _____

Rod _____

Turning point _____

Line of sight _____

Station _____

Height of instrument _____

_____

Unit 61   MATH AIDS IN LEVELING

RELATED INFORMATION

Stations are located and numbered to indicate the position along a pipe line, such as a sewer. The major spacing distance of stations is 100 feet. Plumbing requirements often use 50-foot spacing in leveling. Any distance can be used for a station as needed. The low elevation or other starting point is station 0 + 00. Station 0 + 50 is fifty feet away and station 1 + 00 is 100 feet along the pipe line from station 0 + 00. Station 1 + 27 is 27 feet past station 1 + 00 and 127 feet from station 0 + 00. Numbering the stations in this way is good practice for long distances.

Field notes keep a record of the leveling work and make it possible to check for errors. The field note form and procedure shown in this unit is the result of the experience of many people. Checking for arithmetic errors or procedure errors is readily done to assure accuracy of the results. The use of two lines of notes per station avoids crowding and aids in checking elevations.

SAMPLE PROBLEMS

1. If station 0 + 00 has an elevation of 137.56 feet, determine the elevation of station 0 + 50 when the grade is .01'/ft. (1/8"/ft.)

2. If the instrument height is 143.00 feet, what is the fore sight for station 0 + 50 in problem #1?

SOLUTIONS

1. $.01 \times 50$ = .50 feet

$$137.56$$
$$+ .50$$
$$\overline{138.06} \text{ feet elevation}$$

2. 143.00 feet
$$-138.06$$
$$\overline{4.94} \text{ feet fore sight}$$

ASSIGNMENT

Complete the field notes based on the sketch and items that are completed. The station 0 + 00 stake has been established. The field notes have a check mark for each space in which information items need to be completed. The back sights and fore sights are shown in the sketch. The instrument location is moved to a new position by use of a turning point. The station stakes are firmly driven and each station elevation is 7 feet above the invert of the sewer to be installed. The station number is marked on the stake. The elevation is shown on the stake by a line mark with a nail driven at the correct height.

171

FIELD NOTES

NAMES					DATE
JOB	SEWER FOR JK CO.				
DESCRIPTION OF WORK	SET GRADE STAKES 7 FT. ABOVE INVERT OF SEWER.				
	ELEVATION STAKE AT MAIN SEWER BY CITY SURVEYOR				

STATION	B.S. ( )	H.I.	F.S. (-)	ELEVATION	REMARKS
0 + 00				137.56	On Stake - Set by City Surveyor
	5.44	143.00			137.56 + 5.44
0 + 50				138.06	137.56 + .50
			4.94		143.00 – 138.06
✓		143.00		138.56	
✓		143.00		✓	
			✓		
T.P.		143.00	5.27	✓	At Paint Mark on Boulder
	5.71		✓		
✓				✓	
			✓		
✓				✓	
			✓		
✓				✓	
			✓		

Sketch and Description and Property Location

APPENDIX

The Square Root Tables A through E, pages 175 - 179, give the square roots of numbers from 1.00 — 99.9. By using the same Tables, the square roots of numbers from 100 - 1000 may also be found by proper placement of the decimal point.

EXAMPLE 1:

Find the square root of 105.

The Table shows the square root of 1.05 to be 1.025.

By moving the decimal point one place to the right, we find 10.25 to be the square root of 105.

EXAMPLE 2:

Find the square root of 327.

The Table shows the square root of 3.27 to be 1.808.

Moving the decimal point one place to the right, we find 18.08 to be the square root of 327.

TABLE A

SQUARE ROOT OF NUMBERS 1.00 – 5.49

Number	0	1	2	3	4	5	6	7	8	9
1.0	1.000	1.005̅	1.010	1.015̅	1.020	1.025̅	1.030	1.034	1.039	1.044
1.1	1.049	1.054	1.058̅	1.063	1.068	1.072	1.077	1.082	1.086	1.091
1.2	1.095	1.100	1.105̅	1.109	1.114	1.118	1.122	1.127	1.131	1.136
1.3	1.140	1.145̅	1.149	1.153	1.158	1.162	1.166	1.170	1.175̅	1.179
1.4	1.183	1.187	1.192	1.196	1.200	1.204	1.208	1.212	1.217	1.221
1.5	1.225̅	1.229	1.233	1.237	1.241	1.245̅	1.249	1.253	1.257	1.261
1.6	1.265̅	1.269	1.273	1.277	1.281	1.285̅	1.288	1.292	1.296	1.300
1.7	1.304	1.308	1.311	1.315	1.319	1.323	1.327	1.330	1.334	1.338
1.8	1.342	1.345	1.349	1.353	1.356	1.360	1.364	1.367	1.371	1.375̅
1.9	1.378	1.382	1.386	1.389	1.393	1.396	1.400	1.404	1.407	1.411
2.0	1.414	1.418	1.421	1.425̅	1.428	1.432	1.435	1.439	1.442	1.446
2.1	1.449	1.453	1.456	1.459	1.463	1.466	1.470	1.473	1.476	1.480
2.2	1.483	1.487	1.490	1.493	1.497	1.500	1.503	1.507	1.510	1.513
2.3	1.517	1.520	1.523	1.526	1.530	1.533	1.536	1.539	1.543	1.546
2.4	1.549	1.552	1.556	1.559	1.562	1.565	1.568	1.572	1.575̅	1.578
2.5	1.581	1.584	1.587	1.591	1.594	1.597	1.600	1.603	1.606	1.609
2.6	1.612	1.616	1.619	1.622	1.625̅	1.628	1.631	1.634	1.637	1.640
2.7	1.643	1.646	1.649	1.652	1.655	1.658	1.661	1.664	1.667	1.670
2.8	1.673	1.676	1.679	1.682	1.685	1.688	1.691	1.694	1.697	1.700
2.9	1.703	1.706	1.709	1.712	1.715̅	1.718	1.720	1.723	1.726	1.729
3.0	1.732	1.735̅	1.738	1.741	1.744	1.746	1.749	1.752	1.755̅	1.758
3.1	1.761	1.764	1.766	1.769	1.772	1.775̅	1.778	1.780	1.783	1.786
3.2	1.789	1.792	1.794	1.797	1.800	1.803	1.806	1.808	1.811	1.814
3.3	1.817	1.819	1.822	1.825̅	1.828	1.830	1.833	1.836	1.838	1.841
3.4	1.844	1.847	1.849	1.852	1.855̅	1.857	1.860	1.863	1.865	1.868
3.5	1.871	1.873	1.876	1.879	1.881	1.884	1.887	1.889	1.892	1.895̅
3.6	1.897	1.900	1.903	1.905	1.908	1.910	1.913	1.916	1.918	1.921
3.7	1.924	1.926	1.929	1.931	1.934	1.936	1.939	1.942	1.944	1.947
3.8	1.949	1.952	1.954	1.957	1.960	1.962	1.965̅	1.967	1.970	1.972
3.9	1.975̅	1.977	1.980	1.982	1.985	1.987	1.990	1.992	1.995̅	1.997
4.0	2.000	2.002	2.005̅	2.007	2.010	2.012	2.015̅	2.017	2.020	2.022
4.1	2.025̅	2.027	2.030	2.032	2.035̅	2.037	2.040	2.042	2.045̅	2.047
4.2	2.049	2.052	2.054	2.057	2.059	2.062	2.064	2.066	2.069	2.071
4.3	2.074	2.076	2.078	2.081	2.083	2.086	2.088	2.090	2.093	2.095
4.4	2.098	2.100	2.102	2.105̅	2.107	2.110	2.112	2.114	2.117	2.119
4.5	2.121	2.124	2.126	2.128	2.131	2.133	2.135	2.138	2.140	2.142
4.6	2.145̅	2.147	2.149	2.152	2.154	2.156	2.159	2.161	2.163	2.166
4.7	2.168	2.170	2.173	2.175̅	2.177	2.179	2.182	2.184	2.186	2.189
4.8	2.191	2.193	2.195	2.198	2.200	2.202	2.205	2.207	2.209	2.211
4.9	2.214	2.216	2.218	2.220	2.223	2.225̅	2.227	2.229	2.232	2.234
5.0	2.236	2.238	2.241	2.243	2.245̅	2.247	2.249	2.252	2.254	2.256
5.1	2.258	2.261	2.263	2.265̅	2.267	2.269	2.272	2.274	2.276	2.278
5.2	2.280	2.283	2.285̅	2.287	2.289	2.291	2.293	2.296	2.298	2.300
5.3	2.302	2.304	2.307	2.309	2.311	2.313	2.315	2.317	2.319	2.322
5.4	2.324	2.326	2.328	2.330	2.332	2.335̅	2.337	2.339	2.341	2.343
	0	1	2	3	4	5	6	7	8	9

TABLE B

SQUARE ROOT OF NUMBERS 5.50 - 9.99

Number	0	1	2	3	4	5	6	7	8	9
5.5	2.345	2.347	2.349	2.352	2.354	2.356	2.358	2.360	2.362	2.364
5.6	2.366	2.369	2.371	2.373	2.375̄	2.377	2.379	2.381	2.383	2.385
5.7	2.387	2.390	2.392	2.394	2.396	2.398	2.400	2.402	2.404	2.406
5.8	2.408	2.410	2.412	2.415̄	2.417	2.419	2.421	2.423	2.425̄	2.427
5.9	2.429	2.431	2.433	2.435	2.437	2.439	2.441	2.443	2.445	2.447
6.0	2.449	2.452	2.454	2.456	2.458	2.460	2.462	2.464	2.466	2.468
6.1	2.470	2.472	2.474	2.476	2.478	2.480	2.482	2.484	2.486	2.488
6.2	2.490	2.492	2.494	2.496	2.498	2.500	2.502	2.504	2.506	2.508
6.3	2.510	2.512	2.514	2.516	2.518	2.520	2.522	2.524	2.526	2.528
6.4	2.530	2.532	2.534	2.536	2.538	2.540	2.542	2.544	2.546	2.548
6.5	2.550̄	2.551	2.553	2.555	2.557	2.559	2.561	2.563	2.565	2.567
6.6	2.569	2.571	2.573	2.575̄	2.577	2.579	2.581	2.583	2.585̄	2.587
6.7	2.588	2.590	2.592	2.594	2.596	2.598	2.600	2.602	2.604	2.606
6.8	2.608	2.610	2.612	2.613	2.615	2.617	2.619	2.621	2.623	2.625
6.9	2.627	2.629	2.631	2.632	2.634	2.636	2.638	2.640	2.642	2.644
7.0	2.646	2.648	2.650	2.651	2.653	2.655	2.657	2.659	2.661	2.663
7.1	2.665	2.666	2.668	2.670	2.672	2.674	2.676	2.678	2.680	2.681
7.2	2.683	2.685	2.687	2.689	2.691	2.693	2.694	2.696	2.698	2.700
7.3	2.702	2.704	2.706	2.707	2.709	2.711	2.713	2.715̄	2.717	2.718
7.4	2.720	2.722	2.724	2.726	2.728	2.729	2.731	2.733	2.735̄	2.737
7.5	2.739	2.740	2.742	2.744	2.746	2.748	2.750̄	2.751	2.753	2.755̄
7.6	2.757	2.759	2.760	2.762	2.764	2.766	2.768	2.769	2.771	2.773
7.7	2.775̄	2.777	2.778	2.780	2.782	2.784	2.786	2.787	2.789	2.791
7.8	2.793	2.795̄	2.796	2.798	2.800	2.802	2.804	2.805	2.807	2.809
7.9	2.811	2.812	2.814	2.816	2.818	2.820	2.821	2.823	2.825̄	2.827
8.0	2.828	2.830	2.832	2.834	2.835	2.837	2.839	2.841	2.843	2.844
8.1	2.846	2.848	2.850̄	2.851	2.853	2.855̄	2.857	2.858	2.860	2.862
8.2	2.864	2.865	2.867	2.869	2.871	2.872	2.874	2.876	2.877	2.879
8.3	2.881	2.883	2.884	2.886	2.888	2.890	2.891	2.893	2.895̄	2.897
8.4	2.898	2.900	2.902	2.903	2.905	2.907	2.909	2.910	2.912	2.914
8.5	2.915	2.917	2.919	2.921	2.922	2.924	2.926	2.927	2.929	2.931
8.6	2.933	2.934	2.936	2.938̄	2.939	2.941	2.943	2.944	2.946	2.948
8.7	2.950̄	2.951	2.953	2.955	2.956	2.958̄	2.960	2.961	2.963	2.965̄
8.8	2.966	2.968	2.970	2.972	2.973	2.975̄	2.977	2.978	2.980	2.982
8.9	2.983	2.985̄	2.987	2.988	2.990	2.992	2.993	2.995̄	2.997	2.998
9.0	3.000	3.002	3.003	3.005̄	3.007	3.008	3.010	3.012	3.013	2.015̄
9.1	3.017	3.018	3.020	3.022	3.023	3.025̄	3.027	3.028̄	2.030	3.032
9.2	3.033	3.035̄	3.036	3.038	3.040	3.041	3.043	3.045̄	3.046	3.048
9.3	3.050̄	3.051	3.053	3.055̄	3.056	3.058	3.059	3.061	3.063	3.064
9.4	3.066	3.068	3.069	3.071	3.072	3.074	3.076	3.077	3.079	3.081
9.5	3.082	3.084	3.085	3.087	3.089	3.090	3.092	3.094	3.095	3.097
9.6	3.098	3.100	3.102	3.103	3.105̄	3.106	3.108	3.110	3.111	3.113
9.7	3.114	3.116	3.118	3.119	3.121	3.122	3.124	3.126	3.127	3.129
9.8	3.130	3.132	3.134	3.135	3.137	3.138	3.140	3.142	3.143	3.145̄
9.9	3.146	3.148	3.150̄	3.151	3.153	3.154	3.156	3.158	3.159	3.161
	0	1	2	3	4	5	6	7	8	9

TABLE C

SQUARE ROOT OF NUMBERS   10.0 – 54.9

Number	0	1	2	3	4	5	6	7	8	9
10.	3.162	3.178	3.194	3.209	3.225	3.240	3.256	3.271	3.286	3.302
11.	3.317	3.332	3.347	3.362	3.376	3.391	3.406	3.421	3.435	3.450
12.	3.464	3.479	3.493	3.507	3.521	3.536	3.550	3.564	3.578	3.592
13.	3.606	3.619	3.633	3.647	3.661	3.674	3.688	3.701	3.715	3.728
14.	3.742	3.755	3.768	3.782	3.795	3.808	3.821	3.834	3.847	3.860
15.	3.873	3.886	3.899	3.912	3.924	3.937	3.950	3.962	3.975	3.987
16.	4.000	4.012	4.025	4.037	4.050	4.062	4.074	4.087	4.099	4.111
17.	4.123	4.135	4.147	4.159	4.171	4.183	4.195	4.207	4.219	4.231
18.	4.243	4.254	4.266	4.278	4.290	4.301	4.313	4.324	4.336	4.347
19.	4.359	4.370	4.382	4.393	4.405	4.416	4.427	4.438	4.450	4.461
20.	4.472	4.483	4.494	4.506	4.517	4.528	4.539	4.550	4.561	4.572
21.	4.583	4.593	4.604	4.615	4.626	4.637	4.648	4.658	4.669	4.680
22.	4.690	4.701	4.712	4.722	4.733	4.743	4.754	4.764	4.775	4.785
23.	4.796	4.806	4.817	4.827	4.837	4.848	4.858	4.868	4.879	4.889
24.	4.899	4.909	4.919	4.930	4.940	4.950	4.960	4.970	4.980	4.990
25.	5.000	5.010	5.020	5.030	5.040	5.050	5.060	5.070	5.079	5.089
26.	5.099	5.109	5.119	5.128	5.138	5.148	5.158	5.167	5.177	5.187
27.	5.196	5.206	5.215	5.225	5.235	5.244	5.254	5.263	2.273	5.282
28.	5.292	5.301	5.310	5.320	5.329	5.339	5.348	5.357	5.367	5.376
29.	5.385	5.394	5.404	5.413	5.422	5.431	5.441	5.450	5.459	5.468
30.	5.477	5.486	5.495	5.505	5.514	5.523	5.532	5.541	5.550	5.559
31.	5.568	5.577	5.586	5.595	5.604	5.612	5.621	5.630	5.639	5.648
32.	5.657	5.666	5.675	5.683	5.692	5.701	5.710	5.718	5.727	5.736
33.	5.745	5.753	5.762	5.771	5.779	5.788	5.797	5.805	5.814	5.822
34.	5.831	5.840	5.848	5.857	5.865	5.874	5.882	5.891	5.899	5.908
35.	5.916	5.925	5.933	5.941	5.950	5.958	5.967	5.975	5.983	5.992
36.	6.000	6.008	6.017	6.025	6.033	6.042	6.050	6.058	6.066	6.075
37.	6.083	6.091	6.099	6.107	6.116	6.124	6.132	6.140	6.148	6.156
38.	6.164	6.173	6.181	6.189	6.197	6.205	6.213	6.221	6.229	6.237
39.	6.245	6.253	6.261	6.269	6.277	6.285	6.293	6.301	6.309	6.317
40.	6.325	6.332	6.340	6.348	6.356	6.364	6.372	6.380	6.387	6.395
41.	6.403	6.411	6.419	6.427	6.434	6.442	6.450	6.458	6.465	6.473
42.	6.481	6.488	6.496	6.504	6.512	6.519	6.527	6.535	6.542	6.550
43.	6.557	6.565	6.573	6.580	6.588	6.595	6.603	6.611	6.618	6.626
44.	6.633	6.641	6.648	6.656	6.663	6.671	6.678	6.686	6.693	6.701
45.	6.708	6.716	6.723	6.731	6.738	6.745	6.753	6.760	6.768	6.775
46.	6.782	6.790	6.797	6.804	6.812	6.819	6.826	6.834	6.841	6.848
47.	6.856	6.863	6.870	6.877	6.885	6.892	6.899	6.907	6.914	6.921
48.	6.928	6.935	6.943	6.950	6.957	6.964	6.971	6.979	6.986	6.993
49.	7.000	7.007	7.014	7.021	7.029	7.036	7.043	7.050	7.057	7.064
50.	7.071	7.078	7.085	7.092	7.099	7.106	7.113	7.120	7.127	7.134
51.	7.141	7.148	7.155	7.162	7.169	7.176	7.183	7.190	7.197	7.204
52.	7.211	7.218	7.225	7.232	7.239	7.246	7.253	7.259	7.266	7.273
53.	7.280	7.287	7.294	7.301	7.308	7.314	7.321	7.328	7.335	7.342
54.	7.348	7.355	7.362	7.369	7.376	7.382	7.389	7.396	7.403	7.409
	0	1	2	3	4	5	6	7	8	9

TABLE D

SQUARE ROOT OF NUMBERS 55.0 - 99.9

Numbers	0	1	2	3	4	5	6	7	8	9
55.	7.416	7.423	7.430	7.436	7.443	7.450	7.457	7.463	7.470	7.477
56.	7.483	7.490	7.497	7.503	7.510	7.517	7.523	7.530	7.537	7.543
57.	7.550	7.556	7.563	7.570	7.576	7.583	7.589	7.596	7.603	7.609
58.	7.616	7.622	7.629	7.635	7.642	7.649	7.655	7.662	7.668	7.675
59.	7.681	7.688	7.694	7.701	7.707	7.714	7.720	7.727	7.733	7.740
60.	7.746	7.752	7.759	7.765	7.772	7.778	7.785	7.791	7.797	7.804
61.	7.810	7.817	7.823	7.829	7.836	7.842	7.849	7.855	7.861	7.868
62.	7.874	7.880	7.887	7.893	7.899	7.906	7.912	7.918	7.925	7.931
63.	7.937	7.944	7.950	7.956	7.962	7.969	7.975	7.981	7.987	7.994
64.	8.000	8.006	8.012	8.019	8.025	8.031	8.037	8.044	8.050	8.056
65.	8.062	8.068	8.075	8.081	8.087	8.093	8.099	8.106	8.112	8.118
66.	8.124	8.130	8.136	8.142	8.149	8.155	8.161	8.167	8.173	8.179
67.	8.185	8.191	8.198	8.204	8.210	8.216	8.222	8.228	8.234	8.240
68.	8.246	8.252	8.258	8.264	8.270	8.276	8.283	8.289	8.295	8.301
69.	8.307	8.313	8.319	8.325	8.331	8.337	8.343	8.349	8.355	8.361
70.	8.367	8.373	8.379	8.385	8.390	8.396	8.402	8.408	8.414	8.420
71.	8.426	8.432	8.438	8.444	8.450	8.456	8.462	8.468	8.473	8.479
72.	8.485	8.491	8.497	8.503	8.509	8.515	8.521	8.526	8.532	8.538
73.	8.544	8.550	8.556	8.562	8.567	8.573	8.579	8.585	8.591	8.597
74.	8.602	8.608	8.614	8.620	8.626	8.631	8.637	8.643	8.649	8.654
75.	8.660	8.666	8.672	8.678	8.683	8.689	8.695	8.701	8.706	8.712
76.	8.718	8.724	8.729	8.735	8.741	8.746	8.752	8.758	8.764	8.769
77.	8.775	8.781	8.786	8.792	8.798	8.803	8.809	8.815	8.820	8.826
78.	8.832	8.837	8.843	8.849	8.854	8.860	8.866	8.871	8.877	8.883
79.	8.888	8.894	8.899	8.905	8.911	8.916	8.922	8.927	8.933	8.939
80.	8.944	8.950	8.955	8.961	8.967	8.972	8.978	8.983	8.989	8.994
81.	9.000	9.006	9.011	9.017	9.022	9.028	9.033	9.039	9.044	9.050
82.	9.055	9.061	9.066	9.072	9.077	9.083	9.088	9.094	9.099	9.105
83.	9.110	9.116	9.121	9.127	9.132	9.138	9.143	9.149	9.154	9.160
84.	9.165	9.171	9.176	9.182	9.187	9.192	9.198	9.203	9.209	9.214
85.	9.220	9.225	9.230	9.236	9.241	9.247	9.252	9.257	9.263	9.268
86.	9.274	9.279	9.284	9.290	9.295	9.301	9.306	9.311	9.317	9.322
87.	9.327	9.333	9.338	9.343	9.349	9.354	9.359	9.365	9.370	9.375
88.	9.381	9.386	9.391	9.397	9.402	9.407	9.413	9.418	9.423	9.429
89.	9.434	9.439	9.445	9.450	9.455	9.460	9.466	9.471	9.476	9.482
90.	9.487	9.492	9.497	9.503	9.508	9.513	9.518	9.524	9.529	9.534
91.	9.539	9.545	9.550	9.555	9.560	9.566	9.571	9.576	9.581	9.586
92.	9.592	9.597	9.602	9.607	9.612	9.618	9.623	9.628	9.633	9.638
93.	9.644	9.649	9.654	9.659	9.664	9.670	9.675	9.680	9.685	9.690
94.	9.695	9.701	9.706	9.711	9.716	9.721	9.726	9.731	9.737	9.742
95.	9.747	9.752	9.757	9.762	9.767	9.772	9.778	9.783	9.788	9.793
96.	9.798	9.803	9.808	9.813	9.818	9.823	9.829	9.834	9.839	9.844
97.	9.849	9.854	9.859	9.864	9.869	9.874	9.879	9.884	9.889	9.894
98.	9.899	9.905	9.910	9.915	9.920	9.925	9.930	9.935	9.940	9.945
99.	9.950	9.955	9.960	9.965	9.970	9.975	9.980	9.985	9.990	9.995
	0	1	2	3	4	5	6	7	8	9

TABLE E

POWERS AND ROOTS OF NUMBERS (1 through 100)

Num-ber	Powers		Roots		Num-ber	Powers		Roots	
	Square	Cube	Square	Cube		Square	Cube	Square	Cube
1	1	1	1.000	1.000	51	2,601	132,651	7.141	3.708
2	4	8	1.414	1.260	52	2,704	140,608	7.211	3.733
3	9	27	1.732	1.442	53	2,809	148,877	7.280	3.756
4	16	64	2.000	1.587	54	2,916	157,464	7.348	3.780
5	25	125	2.236	1.710	55	3,025	166,375	7.416	3.803
6	36	216	2.449	1.817	56	3,136	175,616	7.483	3.826
7	49	343	2.646	1.913	57	3,249	185,193	7.550	3.849
8	64	512	2.828	2.000	58	3,364	195,112	7.616	3.871
9	81	729	3.000	2.080	59	3,481	205,379	7.681	3.893
10	100	1,000	3.162	2.154	60	3,600	216,000	7.746	3.915
11	121	1,331	3.317	2.224	61	3,721	226,981	7.810	3.936
12	144	1,728	3.464	2.289	62	3,844	238,328	7.874	3.958
13	169	2,197	3.606	2.351	63	3,969	250,047	7.937	3.979
14	196	2,744	3.742	2.410	64	4,096	262,144	8.000	4.000
15	225	3,375	3.873	2.466	65	4,225	274,625	8.062	4.021
16	256	4,096	4.000	2.520	66	4,356	287,496	8.124	4.041
17	289	4,913	4.123	2.571	67	4,489	300,763	8.185	4.062
18	324	5,832	4.243	2.621	68	4,624	314,432	8.246	4.082
19	361	6,859	4.359	2.668	69	4,761	328,509	8.307	4.102
20	400	8,000	4.472	2.714	70	4,900	343,000	8.367	4.121
21	441	9,261	4.583	2.759	71	5,041	357,911	8.426	4.141
22	484	10,648	4.690	2.802	72	5,184	373,248	8.485	4.160
23	529	12,167	4.796	2.844	73	5,329	389,017	8.544	4.179
24	576	13,824	4.899	2.884	74	5,476	405,224	8.602	4.198
25	625	15,625	5.000	2.924	75	5,625	421,875	8.660	4.217
26	676	17,576	5.099	2.962	76	5,776	438,976	8.718	4.236
27	729	19,683	5.196	3.000	77	5,929	456,533	8.775	4.254
28	784	21,952	5.292	3.037	78	6,084	474,552	8.832	4.273
29	841	24,389	5.385	3.072	79	6,241	493,039	8.888	4.291
30	900	27,000	5.477	3.107	80	6,400	512,000	8.944	4.309
31	961	29,791	5.568	3.141	81	6,561	531,441	9.000	4.327
32	1,024	32,798	5.657	3.175	82	6,724	551,368	9.055	4.344
33	1,089	35,937	5.745	3.208	83	6,889	571,787	9.110	4.362
34	1,156	39,304	5.831	3.240	84	7,056	592,704	9.165	4.380
35	1,225	42,875	5.916	3.271	85	7,225	614,125	9.220	4.397
36	1,296	46,656	6.000	3.302	86	7,396	636,056	9.274	4.414
37	1,369	50,653	6.083	3.332	87	7,569	658,503	9.327	4.481
38	1,444	54,872	6.164	3.362	88	7,744	681,472	9.381	4.448
39	1,521	59,319	6.245	3.391	89	7,921	704,969	9.434	4.465
40	1,600	64,000	6.325	3.420	90	8,100	729,000	9.487	4.481
41	1,681	68,921	6.403	3.448	91	8,281	753,571	9.539	4.498
42	1,764	74,088	6.481	3.476	92	8,464	778,688	9.592	4.514
43	1,849	79,507	6.557	3.503	93	8,649	804,357	9.644	4.531
44	1,936	85,184	6.633	3.530	94	8,836	830,584	9.695	4.547
45	2,025	91,125	6.708	3.557	95	9,025	857,375	9.747	4.563
46	2,116	97,336	6.782	3.583	96	9,216	884,736	9.798	4.579
47	2,209	103,823	6.856	3.609	97	9,409	912,673	9.849	4.595
48	2,304	110,592	6.928	3.634	98	9,604	941,192	9.900	4.610
49	2,401	117,649	7.000	3.659	99	9,801	970,299	9.950	4.626
50	2,500	125,000	7.071	3.684	100	10,000	1,000,000	10.000	4.642

TABLE F
STANDARD TABLES OF ENGLISH MEASURE

Linear Measure	
12 inches (in.)	= 1 foot (ft.)
3 ft.	= 1 yard (yd.)
16 1/2 ft.	= 1 rod (rd.)
5 1/2 yd.	= 1 rd.
320 rd.	= 1 mile
1760 yd.	= 1 mile
5280 ft.	= 1 mile

Surface Measure	
144 sq. in.	= 1 sq. ft.
9 sq. ft.	= 1 sq. yd.
30 1/4 sq. yd.	= 1 sq. rd.
160 sq. rd.	= 1 acre
640 acres	= 1 sq. mile
43,560 sq. ft.	= 1 acre

Cubic Measure	
1728 cu. in.	= 1 cu. ft.
27 cu. ft.	= 1 cu. yd.
128 cu. ft.	= 1 cord

TABLE G
STANDARD TABLES OF METRIC MEASURE

Linear Measure		
Unit	Value in meters	Symbol or Abbrev.
Micron	0.000001	μ
Millimeter	0.001	mm.
Centimeter	0.01	cm.
Decimeter	0.1	dm.
Meter (unit)	1.0	m.
Dekameter	10.0	dkm.
Hectometer	100.0	hm.
Kilometer	1,000.00	km.
Myriameter	10,000.0	Mm.
Megameter	1,000,000.0	

Surface Measure		
Unit	Value in square meters	Symbol or Abbrev
Square millimeter	0.000001	mm.^{2}
Square centimeter	0.0001	cm.^{2}
Square decimeter	0.01	dm.^{2}
Square meter centiare)	1.0	m.^{2}
Square dekameter (are)	100.0	a.^{2}
Hectare	10,000.0	ha.^{2}
Square kilometer	1,000,000.0	km.^{2}

Cubic Measure		
Unit	Value in cubic meters	Symbol or Abbrev.
Cubic micron	10^{-18}	μ^3
Cubic millimeter	10^{-9}	mm.^{3}
Cubic centimeter	10^{-6}	cm.^{3}
Cubic decimeter	10^{-3}	dm.^{3}
Cubic meter	1	m.^{3}
Cubic dekameter	10^3	dkm.^{3}
Cubic hectometer	10^6	hm.^{3}
Cubic kilometer	10^9	km.^{3}

TABLE H
CONVERSION OF ENGLISH AND METRIC MEASURES

	Linear Measure							
Unit	Inches to milli-meters	Milli-meters to inches	Feet to meters	Meters to feet	Yards to meters	Meters to yards	Miles to kilo-meters	Kilo-meters to miles
1	25.40	0.03937	0.3048	3.281	0.9144	1.094	1.609	0.6214
2	50.80	0.07874	0.6096	6.562	1.829	2.187	3.219	1.243
3	76.20	0.1181	0.9144	9.842	2.743	3.281	4.828	1.864
4	101.60	0.1575	1.219	13.12	3.658	4.374	6.437	2.485
5	127.00	0.1968	1.524	16.40	4.572	5.468	8.047	3.107
6	152.40	0.2362	1.829	19.68	5.486	6.562	9.656	3.728
7	177.80	0.2756	2.134	22.97	6.401	7.655	11.27	4.350
8	203.20	0.3150	2.438	26.25	7.315	8.749	12.87	4.971
9	228.60	0.3543	2.743	29.53	8.230	9.842	14.48	5.592
Example	1 in. = 2540 mm.,		1 m. = 3.281 ft.,		1 Km. = 0.6214 mi.			

	Surface Measure									
Unit	Square inches to square centi-meters	Square centi-meters to square inches	Square feet to square meters	Square meters to square feet	Square yards to square meters	Square meters to square yards	Acres to hec-tares	Hec-tares to acres	Square miles to square kilo-meters	Square kilo-meters to square miles
1	6.452	0.1550	0.0929	10.76	0.8361	1.196	0.4047	2.471	2.59	0.3861
2	12.90	0.31	0.1859	21.53	1.672	2.392	0.8094	4.942	5.18	0.7722
3	19.356	0.465	0.2787	32.29	2.508	3.588	1.214	7.413	7.77	1.158
4	25.81	0.62	0.3716	43.06	3.345	4.784	1.619	9.884	10.36	1.544
5	32.26	0.775	0.4645	53.82	4.181	5.98	2.023	12.355	12.95	1.931
6	38.71	0.93	0.5574	64.58	5.017	7.176	2.428	14.826	15.54	2.317
7	45.16	1.085	0.6503	75.35	5.853	8.372	2.833	17.297	18.13	2.703
8	51.61	1.24	0.7432	86.11	6.689	9.568	3.237	19.768	20.72	3.089
9	58.08	1.395	0.8361	96.87	7.525	10.764	3.642	22.239	23.31	3.475
Example	1 sq. in. = 6.452 sq. cm.,		1 sq. m. = 1.196 sq. yds.,		1 sq. mi. = 2.59 sq. Km.					

	Cubic Measure							
Unit	Cubic inches to cubic centi-meters	Cubic centi-meters to cubic inches	Cubic feet to cubic meters	Cubic meters to cubic feet	Cubic yards to cubic meters	Cubic meters to cubic yards	Gallons to cubic feet	Cubic feet to gallons
1	16.39	0.06102	0.02832	35.31	0.7646	1.308	0.1337	7.481
2	32.77	0.1220	0.05663	70.63	1.529	2.616	0.2674	14.96
3	49.16	0.1831	0.08495	105.9	2.294	3.924	0.4010	22.44
4	65.55	0.2441	0.1133	141.3	3.058	5.232	0.5347	29.92
5	81.94	0.3051	0.1416	176.6	3.823	6.540	0.6684	37.40
6	98.32	0.3661	0.1699	211.9	4.587	7.848	0.8021	44.88
7	114.7	0.4272	0.1982	247.2	5.352	9.156	0.9358	52.36
8	131.1	0.4882	0.2265	282.5	6.116	10.46	1.069	59.84
9	147.5	0.5492	0.2549	371.8	6.881	11.77	1.203	67.32
Example	1 cu. cm. = 0.06102 cu. in.,		1 gal. = 0.1337 cu. ft.					

TABLE I

DECIMAL AND MILLIMETER EQUIVALENTS

| Millimeter Equivalents of Decimals (0.01″ to 0.99″) | | | | | | | | | |
Dec.	0	1	2	3	4	5	6	7	8	9
0.0	. . . .	0.254	0.508	0.762	1.016	1.270	1.524	1.778	2.032	2.286
0.1	2.540	2.794	3.048	3.302	3.556	3.810	4.064	4.318	4.572	4.826
0.2	5.080	5.334	5.588	5.842	6.096	6.350	6.604	6.858	7.112	7.366
0.3	7.620	7.874	8.128	8.392	8.636	8.890	9.144	9.398	9.652	9.906
0.4	10.160	10.414	10.688	10.922	11.176	11.430	11.684	11.938	12.192	12.446
0.5	12.700	12.954	13.208	13.462	13.716	13.970	14.224	14.478	14.732	14.986
0.6	15.240	15.494	15.748	16.022	16.256	16.510	16.764	17.018	17.272	17.526
0.7	17.780	18.034	18.288	18.542	18.796	19.050	19.304	19.558	19.812	20.066
0.8	20.320	20.574	20.828	21.082	21.336	21.590	21.844	22.098	22.352	22.606
0.9	22.860	23.114	23.368	23.622	23.876	24.130	24.384	24.638	24.892	25.146

Example   0.1″ = 2.540 mm., 0.75″ = 19.050 mm.

| Decimal Equivalents of Millimeters (1 mm. to 99 mm.) | | | | | | | | | |
Mm.	0	1	2	3	4	5	6	7	8	9
0	. . . .	0.0394	0.0787	0.1181	0.1575	0.1968	0.2362	0.2756	0.3150	0.3543
1	0.3937	0.4331	0.4724	0.5118	0.5512	0.5906	0.6299	0.6693	0.7087	0.7480
2	0.7874	0.8268	0.8661	0.9055	0.9449	0.9842	1.0236	1.0630	1.1024	1.1417
3	1.1811	1.2205	1.2598	1.2992	1.3386	1.3780	1.4173	1.4567	1.4961	1.5354
4	1.5748	1.6142	1.6535	1.6929	1.7323	1.7716	1.8110	1.8504	1.8898	1.9291
5	1.9685	2.0079	2.0472	2.0866	2.1260	2.1654	2.2047	2.2441	2.2835	2.3228
6	2.3622	2.4016	2.4409	2.4803	2.5197	2.5590	2.5984	2.6378	2.6772	2.7165
7	2.7559	2.7953	2.8346	2.8740	2.9134	2.9528	2.9921	3.0315	3.0709	3.1102
8	3.1496	3.1890	3.2283	3.2677	3.3071	3.3464	3.3858	3.4252	3.4646	3.5039
9	3.5433	3.5827	3.6220	3.6614	3.7008	3.7402	3.7795	3.8189	3.8583	3.8976

Example   10 mm. = 0.3937″,   57 mm. = 2.2441″

DATA 1

STANDARD WEIGHT PIPE – Diameters, Threads

Nominal Size	Diameters (in inches)				Threads			
	O.D.	I.D.	Wood Auger for Pipe	Tap Drill	Number per Inch	Length on Pipe	Threads on Pipe	Thread-in
$\frac{1}{8}$	.405	.269	$\frac{1}{2}$	$\frac{21}{64}$	27	$\frac{3''}{8}$	10	$\frac{1''}{4}$
$\frac{1}{4}$	.540	.364	$\frac{5}{8}$	$\frac{29}{64}$	18	$\frac{9''}{16}$	10	$\frac{3''}{8}$
$\frac{3}{8}$	.675	.493	$\frac{11}{16}$	$\frac{19}{32}$	18	$\frac{9''}{16}$	10	$\frac{3''}{8}$
$\frac{1}{2}$	.840	.622	$\frac{15}{16}$	$\frac{23}{32}$	14	$\frac{3''}{4}$	$10\frac{1}{2}$	$\frac{1''}{2}$
$\frac{3}{4}$	1.050	.824	$1\frac{1}{8}$	$\frac{15}{16}$	14	$\frac{3''}{4}$	$10\frac{1}{2}$	$\frac{1''}{2}$
1	1.315	1.049	$1\frac{7}{16}$	$1\frac{3}{16}$	$11\frac{1}{2}$	$1''$	$11\frac{1}{2}$	$\frac{1''}{2}$
$1\frac{1}{4}$	1.660	1.380	$1\frac{3}{4}$	$1\frac{15}{16}$	$11\frac{1}{2}$	$1''$	$11\frac{1}{2}$	$\frac{1''}{2}$
$1\frac{1}{2}$	1.900	1.610	2	$1\frac{23}{32}$	$11\frac{1}{2}$	$1''$	$11\frac{1}{2}$	$\frac{1''}{2}$
2	2.375	2.067	$2\frac{1}{2}$	$2\frac{3}{16}$	$11\frac{1}{2}$	$1''$	$11\frac{1}{2}$	$\frac{1''}{2}$
$2\frac{1}{2}$	2.875	2.469	3	$2\frac{5}{8}$	8	$1\frac{1''}{2}$	12	$\frac{3''}{4}$
3	3.500	3.068	$3\frac{11}{16}$	$3\frac{1}{4}$	8	$1\frac{1''}{2}$	12	$1''$
$3\frac{1}{2}$	4.000	3.548	$4\frac{1}{4}$	$3\frac{3}{4}$	8	$1\frac{5''}{8}$	13	$1''$
4	4.500	4.025	$4\frac{11}{16}$	$4\frac{1}{4}$	8	$1\frac{5''}{8}$	13	$1''$
5	5.563	5.047	$5\frac{3}{4}$	$5\frac{5}{16}$	8	$1\frac{3''}{4}$	14	$1\frac{1''}{4}$
6	6.625	6.065	$6\frac{7}{8}$	$6\frac{5}{16}$	8	$1\frac{3''}{4}$	14	$1\frac{1''}{4}$
8	8.625	7.981	$8\frac{7}{8}$	$8\frac{3}{8}$	8	$2''$	16	$1\frac{1''}{4}$
10	10.75	10.02	11	$10\frac{5}{8}$	8	$2''$	16	$1\frac{1''}{2}$
12	12.75	12.00	13	$12\frac{5}{8}$	8	$2\frac{1''}{2}$	20	$1\frac{5''}{8}$

DATA 2

THREADED ELBOWS

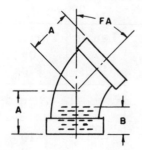

FA is Fitting Angle

A is Center-to-Face Measure

B is Thread-in Measure

Nominal Pipe Size	A Fitting Angles					B
	90°	60°	45°	22 1/2°	11 1/4°	
$\frac{3''}{8}$	$1''$		$\frac{3''}{4}$			$\frac{3''}{8}$
$\frac{1''}{2}$	$1\frac{1''}{8}$		$\frac{3''}{4}$			$\frac{1''}{2}$
$\frac{3''}{4}$	$1\frac{3''}{8}$		$1''$			$\frac{1''}{2}$
$1''$	$1\frac{1''}{2}$		$1\frac{1''}{8}$			$\frac{1''}{2}$
$1\frac{1''}{4}$	$1\frac{3''}{4}$	$1\frac{1''}{4}$	$1\frac{1''}{4}$	$1\frac{1''}{8}$	$1''$	$\frac{1''}{2}$
$1\frac{1''}{2}$	$1\frac{7''}{8}$	$1\frac{3''}{4}$	$1\frac{1''}{2}$	$1\frac{1''}{4}$	$1\frac{1''}{8}$	$\frac{1''}{2}$
$2''$	$2\frac{1''}{4}$	$2\frac{1''}{4}$	$1\frac{5''}{8}$	$1\frac{3''}{8}$	$1\frac{1''}{4}$	$\frac{1''}{2}$
$2\frac{1''}{2}$	$2\frac{3''}{4}$	$2\frac{1''}{2}$	$1\frac{3''}{4}$	$1\frac{1''}{2}$	$1\frac{3''}{8}$	$\frac{3''}{4}$

Use this data for the problems in this book.
Measure fittings on the job.

DATA 3

THREADED TEES

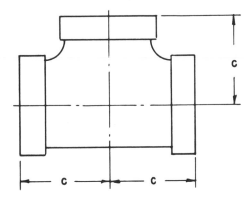

C is Center-to-Face
Measure

B is the Thread-in

Nominal Pipe Size	C	B
$\frac{3''}{8}$	$1''$	$\frac{3''}{8}$
$\frac{1''}{2}$	$1\frac{1''}{8}$	$\frac{1''}{2}$
$\frac{3''}{4}$	$1\frac{3''}{8}$	$\frac{1''}{2}$
$1''$	$1\frac{1''}{2}$	$\frac{1''}{2}$
$1\frac{1''}{4}$	$1\frac{3''}{4}$	$\frac{1''}{2}$
$1\frac{1''}{2}$	$1\frac{7''}{8}$	$\frac{1''}{2}$
$2''$	$2\frac{1''}{4}$	$\frac{1''}{2}''$
$2 \times 1\frac{1''}{2}$	$2\frac{1''}{4}$	$\frac{1''}{2}$
$2\frac{1''}{2}$	$2\frac{3''}{4}$	$\frac{3''}{4}$

Use this data for the problems in this book.
Measure fittings on the job.

DATA 4

THREADED WYE – 45° Fitting Angle

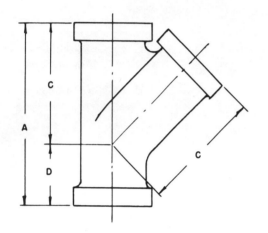

A is Face-to-Face

C is Center-to-Face

D is Center-to-Face

B is Thread-in

Nominal Pipe Size	A	C	D	B
$1\frac{1}{2}''$	$4\frac{3}{4}''$	$3\frac{5}{16}''$	$1\frac{7}{16}''$	$\frac{1}{2}''$
$2''$	$5\frac{7}{8}''$	$4\frac{1}{16}''$	$1\frac{13}{16}''$	$\frac{1}{2}''$
$2'' \times 1\frac{1}{2}''$	$5\frac{7}{8}''$	$4\frac{1}{4}''$	$1\frac{5}{8}''$	$\frac{1}{2}''$
$2\frac{1}{2}'' \times 2''$	$6\frac{1}{4}''$	$4\frac{5}{8}''$	$1\frac{5}{8}''$	$\frac{3}{4}'' \times \frac{1}{2}''$

Use this data for the problems in this book.
Measure fittings on the job.

DATA 5

THREADED TEE-WYE 90° Fitting Angle

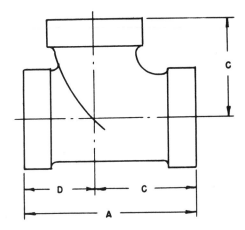

A is Face-to-Face

C is Center-to-Face

D is Center-to-Face

B is Thread-in

Nominal Pipe Size	A	C	D	B
$1\frac{1}{2}''$	$4\frac{1}{4}''$	$2\frac{1}{2}''$	$1\frac{3}{4}''$	$\frac{1}{2}''$
$2''$	$5\frac{1}{8}''$	$2\frac{7}{8}''$	$2\frac{1}{4}''$	$\frac{1}{2}''$
$2'' \times 1\frac{1}{2}''$	$4\frac{1}{2}''$	$2\frac{3}{4}''$	$1\frac{3}{4}''$	$\frac{1}{2}''$
$2\frac{1}{2}'' \times 2''$	$5\frac{7}{16}''$	$3\frac{1}{4}''$	$2\frac{3}{16}''$	$\frac{3}{4}'' \times \frac{1}{2}''$

Use this data for the problems in this book.
Measure fittings on the job.

DATA 6

DECIMAL – FRACTIONAL EQUIVALENTS, INCHES

Decimal	Fraction	Limits
.000	0	.000 - .031
.062	1/16	.032 - .093
.125	1/8	.094 - .156
.187	3/16	.157 - .218
.25	1/4	.219 - .281
.312	5/16	.282 - .343
.375	3/8	.344 - .406
.437	7/16	.407 - .468
.5	1/2	.469 - .531
.562	9/16	.532 - .593
.625	5/8	.594 - .656
.687	11/16	.657 - .718
.75	3/4	.719 - .781
.812	13/16	.782 - .843
.875	7/8	.844 - .906
.937	15/16	.907 - .968
1.000	16/16	.969 - 1.031

DATA 7
CONSTANTS FOR 45° FITTINGS

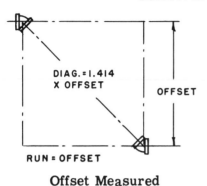

Offset Measured

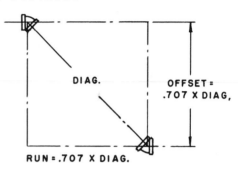

Diagonal Measured

DATA 8
CONSTANTS FOR 60° FITTINGS

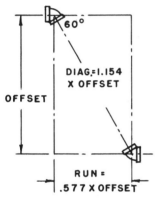

Offset Measured

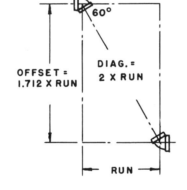

Run Measured

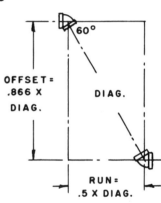

Diagonal Measured

DATA 9
CONSTANTS FOR 22 1/2° FITTINGS

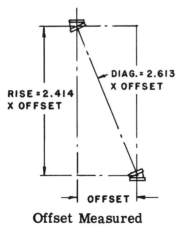

Offset Measured

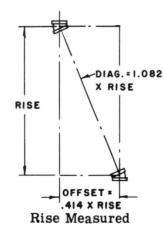

Rise Measured

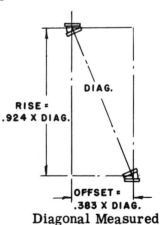

Diagonal Measured

189

DATA 10
CONSTANTS FOR 11 1/4° FITTINGS

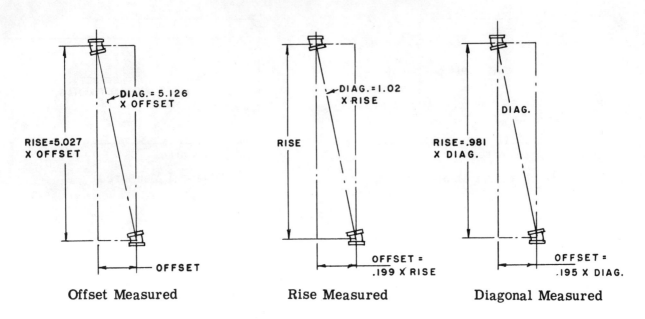

Offset Measured   Rise Measured   Diagonal Measured

DATA 11
CONSTANTS FOR 1/5 BENDS

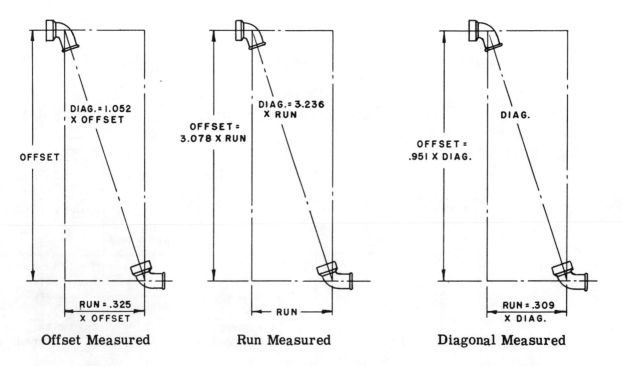

Offset Measured   Run Measured   Diagonal Measured

DATA 12
1/4 BEND

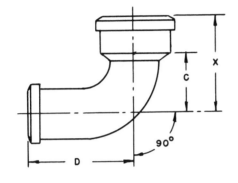

Size	D	C	X	Weight
2	6	$3\frac{1}{4}$	$5\frac{3}{4}$	5
3	7	4	$6\frac{3}{4}$	10
4	8	$4\frac{1}{2}$	$7\frac{1}{2}$	15

Dimensions in inches
Weight in pounds

DATA 13
1/5 BEND

Size	D	C	X	Weight
2	$5\frac{1}{4}$	$2\frac{1}{2}$	5	5
3	6	3	$5\frac{3}{4}$	10
4	7	$3\frac{1}{2}$	$6\frac{1}{2}$	14

Dimensions in inches
Weight in pounds

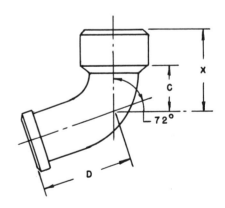

DATA 14
1/6 BEND

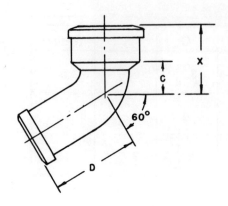

Size	D	C	X	Weight
2	$4\frac{3}{4}$	2	$4\frac{1}{2}$	5
3	$5\frac{1}{2}$	$2\frac{1}{2}$	$5\frac{1}{4}$	9
4	$6\frac{1}{4}$	$2\frac{3}{4}$	$5\frac{3}{4}$	13

Dimensions in inches
Weight in pounds

DATA 15
1/8 BEND

Size	D	C	X	Weight
2	$4\frac{1}{4}$	$1\frac{1}{2}$	4	4
3	5	2	$4\frac{3}{4}$	8
4	$5\frac{3}{4}$	$2\frac{1}{4}$	$5\frac{1}{4}$	12

Dimensions in inches
Weight in pounds

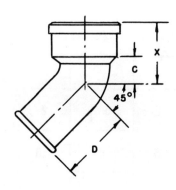

DATA 16
1/16 BEND

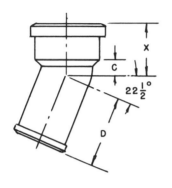

Size	D	C	X	Weight
2	$3\frac{5}{8}$	$\frac{7}{8}$	$3\frac{3}{8}$	4
3	$4\frac{1}{4}$	$1\frac{1}{4}$	4	8
4	$4\frac{3}{4}$	$1\frac{1}{4}$	$4\frac{1}{4}$	11

Dimensions in inches
Weight in pounds

DATA 17
SINGLE AND DOUBLE WYE BRANCHES

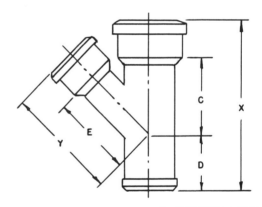

Dimensions in inches
Weight in pounds

Size	D	C	X	E	Y	Weight
2	4	4	$10\frac{1}{2}$	4	$6\frac{1}{2}$	8
3	5	$5\frac{1}{2}$	$13\frac{1}{4}$	$5\frac{1}{2}$	$8\frac{1}{4}$	17
4	$5\frac{1}{4}$	$6\frac{3}{4}$	15	$6\frac{3}{4}$	$9\frac{3}{4}$	24
3×2	$4\frac{1}{4}$	$4\frac{3}{4}$	$11\frac{3}{4}$	5	$7\frac{1}{2}$	14
4×2	$3\frac{5}{8}$	$5\frac{3}{8}$	12	$5\frac{3}{4}$	$8\frac{1}{4}$	17

DATA 18
SINGLE AND DOUBLE SANITARY TEE (TY) BRANCHES

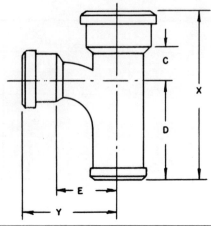

Dimensions in inches
Weight in pounds

Size	D	C	X	E	Y	Weight
2	$6\frac{1}{4}$	$1\frac{3}{4}$	$10\frac{1}{2}$	$2\frac{3}{4}$	$5\frac{1}{4}$	8
3	$7\frac{1}{2}$	$2\frac{1}{2}$	$12\frac{3}{4}$	4	$6\frac{3}{4}$	16
4	8	3	14	$4\frac{1}{2}$	$7\frac{1}{2}$	22
3×2	7	2	$11\frac{3}{4}$	4	$6\frac{1}{2}$	14
4×2	7	2	12	$4\frac{1}{2}$	7	17

DATA 19
SINGLE AND DOUBLE TAPPED TEE BRANCHES

Size	D	C	E	X	Weight
2×2	$6\frac{1}{4}$	$1\frac{3}{4}$	2	$10\frac{1}{2}$	8
$3\times1\frac{1}{2}$, 3×2	7	2	$2\frac{1}{2}$	$11\frac{3}{4}$	13
$4\times1\frac{1}{2}$, 4×2	7	2	3	12	17

Dimensions in inches
Weight in pounds

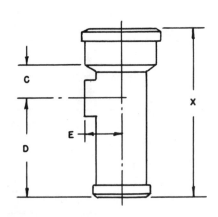

DATA 20
SLIP AND CAULK TYPE DRAINAGE FITTINGS

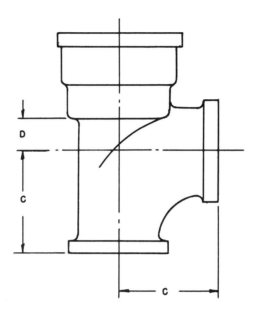

Pipe Size	D	C	B
$1\frac{1}{2}$	$\frac{3}{4}$	$2\frac{3}{4}$	$\frac{1}{2}$
2	$\frac{3}{4}$	3	$\frac{1}{2}$

Use this data for the problems in this book.
Measure fittings on the job.

DATA 21
STANDARD WEIGHT PIPE – Diameters, Capacities

Nominal Diameter	Actual I. D.	Actual O.D.	Outside Circum. Inches	Outside Circum. Feet	Inside Area Sq. In.	Inside Area Sq. Ft.	Sq. Ft. O.D.Area Lin. Ft.	Gallons Lin.Ft.	Pounds Water Lin.Ft.	Wt.Pipe (Lbs.) Lin.Ft.
1/8	.269	.405	1.272	.106	.057	.0004	.106	.003	.024	.246
1/4	.364	.540	1.696	.141	.104	.0007	.141	.005	.045	.426
3/8	.493	.675	2.121	.177	.191	.0013	.177	.009	.082	.570
1/2	.622	.840	2.639	.220	.304	.0021	.220	.015	.131	.855
3/4	.824	1.050	3.299	.273	.533	.0037	.273	.027	.230	1.140
1	1.049	1.315	4.131	.343	.864	.006	.343	.044	.374	1.690
1 1/4	1.388	1.660	5.215	.433	1.496	.0103	.433	.077	.647	2.290
1 1/2	1.610	1.900	5.969	.497	2.036	.0141	.497	.105	.881	2.740
2	2.067	2.375	7.461	.622	3.356	.023	.622	.174	1.453	3.690
2 1/2	2.469	2.875	9.032	.751	4.778	.033	.751	.248	2.073	5.85
3	3.068	3.500	11.00	.843	7.393	.051	.843	.384	3.201	7.66
3 1/2	3.548	4.000	12.566	1.045	9.90	.068	1.045	.515	4.290	8.98
4	4.026	4.500	14.14	1.18	12.73	.088	1.178	.661	5.512	10.9
5	5.047	5.563	17.49	1.455	20.01	.139	1.455	1.039	8.662	14.9
6	6.065	6.625	20.81	1.73	28.89	.2	1.734	1.500	12.51	19.2
8	7.981	8.625	27.10	2.26	50.03	.35	2.258	2.598	21.66	28.9
10	10.020	10.750	33.772	2.81	78.85	.545	2.81	4.096	34.12	40.5
12	12.000	12.750	40.055	3.38	113.09	.984	3.38	5.88	48.96	49.56

DATA 22
CONSTANTS FOR PARALLEL OFFSETS

Fitting Angle	90°	72°	60°	45°	$22\frac{1}{2}$°	$11\frac{1}{4}$°
Diagonal = Offset ×	--	1.052	1.154	1.414	2.613	5.126
Rise (Run) = Offset ×	--	.325	.577	1.	2.414	5.027
Parallel Angle	45°	36°	30°	$22\frac{1}{2}$°	$11\frac{1}{4}$°	$5\frac{5}{8}$°
Difference in Length = Spread ×	1.	.727	.577	.414	.199	.098

DATA 23
CONSTANTS FOR ROLLING OFFSETS

Fitting Angle	90°	72°	60°	45°	$22\frac{1}{2}$°	$11\frac{1}{4}$°
Diagonal	1	1.052	1.154	1.414	2.613	5.126
Setback	0	.325	.577	1.	2.414	5.027

197

DATA 24
COPPER TUBES – DIAMETERS

Nominal Size (in.)	Outside Dia. (in.) Types K, L, M, D.W.V.	Inside Diameter (in.)			
		Type K	Type L	Type M	Type D.W.V.
1/4	0.375	0.305	0.315		
3/8	0.500	0.402	0.430		
1/2	0.625	0.527	0.545		
5/8	0.750	0.652	0.666		
3/4	0.875	0.745	0.785		
1	1.125	0.995	1.025		
1 1/4	1.375	1.245	1.265	1.291	1.295
1 1/2	1.625	1.481	1.505	1.527	1.511
2	2.125	1.959	1.985	2.009	2.041
2 1/2	2.625	2.435	2.465	2.495	
3	3.125	2.907	2.945	2.981	3.035
3 1/2	3.625	3.385	3.425	3.459	
4	4.125	3.857	3.905	3.935	4.009
5	5.125	4.805	4.875	4.907	4.981
6	6.125	5.741	5.845	5.881	5.959
8	8.125	7.583	7.725	7.785	
10	10.125	9.449	9.625	9.701	
12	12.125	11.315	11.565	11.617	

DATA 25
COPPER ELBOWS

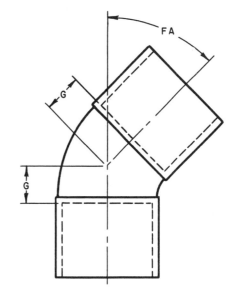

FA - is fitting angle.

G - is allowance for fitting.

Nominal Tube Size	G Fitting Angles				
	90°	60°	45°	22 1/2°	11 1/4°
3/8″	5/16″		3/16″		
1/2″	3/8″		3/16″		
3/4″	1/2″		1/4″		
1″	3/4″		5/16″		
1 1/4″	7/8″	5/8″	7/16″	3/16″	1/8″
1 1/2″	15/16″	3/4″	1/2″	1/4″	1/8″
2	1 1/4″	1 1/16″	1/2″	8/8″	3/16″
2 1/2″	1 1/2″		5/8″		
3″	2 15/16″	1 11/16″	1 3/16″	9/16″	1/4″
4″	3 7/8″	2 1/4″	1 5/8″	3/4″	5/16″

DATA 26

COPPER WYE – 45° FITTING ANGLE

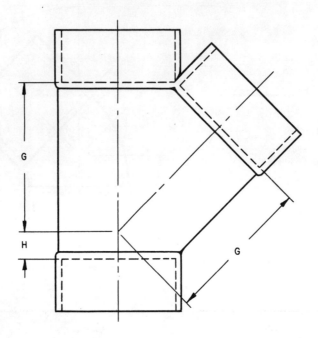

G — is allowance for fitting long center run or branch.

H — is allowance for fitting short center on run.

Nominal Tube Size	G	H
1 1/2″	2 3/16″	3/8″
2″	2 3/4″	9/16″
2″ × 1 1/2″	2 9/16″	1/4″
2 1/2″ × 2″		
3″	4 1/8″	13/16″
4″	5 3/8″	1 1/16″

DATA 27
COPPER TEE-WYE OR 90° SANITARY TEE

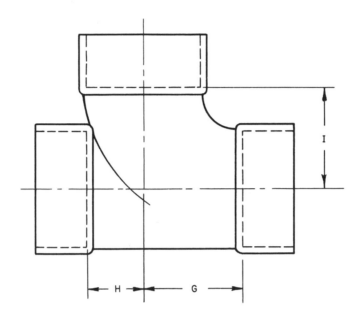

Nominal Tube Size	G	H	I
1 1/2"	1 7/16"	13/16"	1 7/16"
2"	1 15/16"	1"	1 15/16"
2" × 1 1/2"	1 7/16"	13/16"	1 11/16"
2 1/2" × 2"			
3"	2 15/16"	1 1/2"	2 15/16"
4"	3 7/8"	1 15/16"	3 7/8"

DATA 28
NO-HUB CAST IRON BENDS

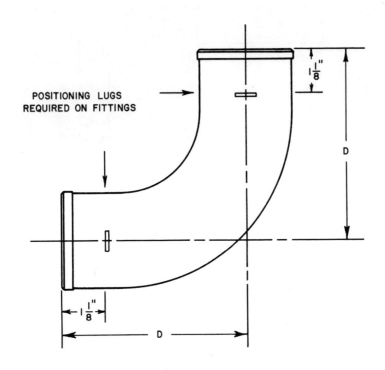

D - Laying Lengths (in inches)

	Bends				
Pipe Size	1/4	1/5	1/6	1/8	1/16
2	4 1/2	3 11/16	3 1/4	2 3/4	2 1/8
3	5	4 1/16	3 1/2	3	2 1/4
4	5 1/2	4 7/16	3 13/16	3 1/8	2 5/16

281(0C1016)